TERRY SUTTON

THE DOVECOTE PRESS

For Family and Friends

First published in 2010 by The Dovecote Press Ltd
Stanbridge, Wimborne Minster, Dorset BH21 4JD

ISBN 978-1-904-34986-0

© Terry Sutton 2010

The author has asserted his rights under the Copyright, Designs
and Patent Act 1988 to be identified as author of this work

Designed by The Dovecote Press
Printed and bound in Singapore by KHL Printing Ltd

All papers used by The Dovecote Press are natural,
recyclable products made from wood grown in sustainable,
well-managed forests

A CIP catalogue record for this book is available
from the British Library

1 3 5 7 9 8 6 4 2

*In the mid-1400s Joannes Gutenberg made printing from moveable type practical
for the first time. Letterpress printing is rightly regarded as one of the world's greatest
inventions. The first all-metal presses were introduced in the early part of the
nineteenth century. The 'Wharfedale' cylinder letterpress printing machine shown
on the left, was made by W. Dawson & Sons, Otley in the 1890s. Photographs
reproduced by courtesy of the Bradford Industrial Museum.*

CONTENTS

ACKNOWLEDGEMENTS

Back in 2003 I first set eyes upon 'the slotter', a machine tool made in Keighley a century ago, and now on display at the Bradford Industrial Museum. It might not have been love at first sight, but the moment became the unlikely starting point for what has since been a fascinating and enlightening odyssey down a few avenues of Yorkshire's industrial past. The inevitable involvement of others along the way has provided an added bonus.

My warmest thanks go to; Mike Bruce, for his guidance with the text; the digital expertise of Chris Wainwright; and John Holroyd for his contribution to the book from his matchless photo archive. Julie Hilditch, Keith Orange, Caron Naylor, Warren Sykes, Mike Oliver and Tony Mellor have, as always, provided motivation and support throughout the book's lengthy progress.

A number of my own photographs were taken with permission and assistance from; Tony Sharpe, Shibden Hall Museum, Halifax; Staff at Bradford Industrial Museum; Richard Macfarlane and Jeff Wilkinson, Calderdale Museums and Galleries; The SDC Colour Museum, Bradford; The National Coalmining Museum for England; Adrian Marshall, Mike Riches, Thwaite Mills Watermill, Leeds; Dewsbury Minster; Birstall St Peter; All Saints Parish Church, Ilkley; The Museum of East Riding Rural Life, Skidby. John Goodchild, M.Univ., Norman Ellis, John Crawley, Alan Whitworth and Gloria Wilson have allowed me to produce illustrations based on photographs from their archives.

My thanks to the following who have searched their archives, and/or given me information and encouragement through their interest: Graham Alcock, Caroline Benson, Amanda Booth, Roger Birch, Robert Blackburn, F.R.H.S., Jackie Cook, Michael Callaghan, Peter Dick, Neil Dowlan, Brian Elliott, Kenneth Elliff, Nicola Fox, John D. Griffin, Steve Gillard, Edward Howard, Jackie Logan, Ian Macdonald, Shirley Miller, Gavin Morrison, Eugene Nicholson, Emma Paragreen, Jenny Parker, Jeff Poar, Max Priestley, Maggie Peddley, Mr. and Mrs. A Pinchin, Peter Rix, Andrew Robinson, Michael J. Shaw, Brian Steptoe, Steve Tagg, Peter Tuffrey, Helen Wallder, Helen Walsh, Mrs. Dorothy Whitaker, Gloria Wilson, Ruby Wills, Frank Woolrych, Yorkshire Gliding Club, Copy Concept, Cleckheaton. The brass plate for the cover of the book was cast by Procast of Heckmondwike.

Finally, my gratitude to my family for their patience and tolerance and my publisher David Burnett for channelling the efforts of myself and others into what I hope is a worthy tribute to Yorkshire's capacity for HARD GRAFT.

TERRY SUTTON
Cleckheaton 2010

PICTURE CREDITS

INTRODUCTION

Quite how I once managed to come fourth in my class in woodwork now leaves me somewhat baffled. But the evidence is plain to see in my end of year Secondary Modern school report for July 1955. Time has now proved conclusively that the word 'adequate' would best describe my excursions into the world of practical construction and repairs, confirming that a future career as a carpenter, stonemason or engineer would, for me, never be in the scheme of things.

Art was always my strongest subject at school. After leaving the School of Art & Design, Batley, I pursued a career as a graphic designer but found myself drawn more and more towards illustration, aided and abetted by a growing interest in photography.

In the 1950s I developed a fascination for railway locomotives (a not unusual trait for boys at the time). This was of course in the days when steam hauled trains were an everyday occurrence on our railways. My interest in art led to a more challenging objective, that of drawing and painting these wonderful machines.

Complicated valve gear, wheels and boilers with intimidating ellipses were tackled with youthful enthusiasm. Before the more enlightening experience of art school, landscape and architecture were treated as mere background subject matter. In retrospect, steam locomotives played an early and significant part in my career in art and design.

History and 'heritage' now endorse that some man-made objects built primarily for a particular purpose are now considered as works of art. The Motive Power Gallery at the Bradford Industrial Museum houses a fine collection of working stationary steam engines – once the pride of the mills and factories for which they provided the power. Among this display of gleaming paintwork and polished brass and copper is a group of machines occupying a decidedly more mundane world. Very few of the lathes, drills and other machine tools in this, the 'mechanics shop' section of the display, would warrant a second glance. By turning my

First sunk in 1903, all traces of Shaw Cross Colliery near Dewsbury, have now completely disappeared. Based on an art college sketchbook drawing from November 11th 1961.

back on the obvious I found the inspiration for this, my second book –
'HARD GRAFT'.

Painted unlined plain black, but with the pleasing surface patina of a
much used machine, stood the 'slotter' or combined machine. Destined to
serve industry away from the public gaze – but appreciated never the less
by those who daily used it – this dour industrial workhorse was designed
and built to carry out a fundamental engineering process; whereby, wheels
and pulleys were secured to their shafts by driving a square sectioned
metal wedge into a matching groove or 'keyway' cut into both wheel and
shaft. In other words *a machine that made machines,* without which the
stellar examples of Victorian and Edwardian steam power nearby would
have never got further than the drawing office stage.

The team of engineers at J & S Smith, Keighley, who built the 'slotter'
in the early part of the twentieth century would no doubt have been
bemused at any attempt to endow this product of their labours with
artistic pretentions, but in justification, machinery and machine tools are
no strangers to exhibition halls.

During the nineteenth century, Britain acquired a reputation as 'the
workshop of the world'. Industrialists were quick to capitalise on this
growing reputation. The 'workshop' needed a shop window. In 1851 this
was duly delivered in London's Hyde Park. Joseph Paxton's great cathedral
of iron and glass – named the 'Crystal Palace' by *Punch* magazine – allowed
manufacturers and the general public to justifiably bask in a breathtaking
display of Britain's industrial ingenuity and progress.

What can only be described as exhibition fever quickly followed; not
only in Britain but throughout the growing industrial world, including:
Paris, 1855/1867; Vienna, 1873; Philadelphia, 1876 and Melbourne,
1881. Yorkshire companies came away with gold and silver medals from
all these and other events closer to home, where exhibitions were held in
Leeds, 1875; Huddersfield, 1883; Sheffield, 1885 and Bradford, 1893/
1904. In the latter half of the nineteenth century, textile machinery,
railway locomotives and pottery were among the growing number of
products being exported by Yorkshire manufacturers to destinations
throughout the world.

Smoke from coal-fired furnaces and the homes of an expanding
population became ever more pervasive over large areas of Yorkshire –
the price to pay for the hope of a more prosperous future. That anything
sublime could emerge from this stygian gloom is best illustrated by areas
of industrial Yorkshire where factory potteries contributed to the smoky
pallor along the banks of the rivers' Aire, Calder, Don and Tees. Here

*A corn flail and a pair of cropping shears decorate a carved bench end in the church
of Birstall St Peter near Batley. Carved in 1616, they represent the tools of the
owner's trade at a time when agriculture and wool were important to England's
domestic economy and overseas trade. In later centuries in Yorkshire, artistry and
craftsmanship in wood attained national and international recognition through the
work of Otley born, Thomas Chippendale (1718-1779) and Robert Thompson of
Kilburn (1876-1955).*

objects of exquisite beauty were created amidst the abrasive clamour of
mining and heavy industries.

This striking blend of contrasts personifies the richness and variety of
Yorkshire's craft skills and industrial achievements; a county which has
nurtured such diverse talents as furniture maker; Thomas Chippendale,
engineer John Smeaton and 'Catseye' reflecting road stud inventor, Percy
Shaw. Individual craftspeople like clock makers, organ builders, tailors
and potters have all found their niche in the shadow of the great industries
of mass production employing thousands.

A monument in the churchyard of Kirkheaton St John, near
Huddersfield, commemorates the deaths of 17 girls aged between 9 and
18 who, on the night of February 14th 1818, perished in a fire which
swept through a cotton mill at nearby Colne Bridge. Flames quickly

Prize Medal awarded at the Bradford Fine Art and Industrial Exhibition of 1882, held at Bradford Technical College.

THE 'SLOTTER'
A MACHINE THAT MADE MACHINES

Alongside lathes, drilling machines, grinders and gear cutters, the 'Slotter' or combined machine is among the unsung engineering tools that have created many of the artefacts that bring pride and admiration to our industrial achievements.

Devoid of any whimsical appendages immaterial to functionality, machine tools are what they are because of what they do — you could say; aesthetics in its purest form.

Designed and built by an engineering company in Keighley at the turn of the twentieth century, the 'Slotter' was never intended to be seen as a work of art. Now on display at the Bradford Industrial Museum, it is time to appreciate this aspect of our industrial past and recognise that this modest machine is maybe only a few steps away from the accolades conferred upon the likes of the 'Flying Scotsman', Jowett Javelin, the windmill at Skidby, finely crafted clocks and musical instruments, or the sculptures of Henry Moore and Barbara Hepworth.

destroyed an internal stairway, leaving the girls with no chance of escape. Stories that the girls were trapped in a room to which the key had been mislaid have since been refuted.

This tragic story is a compelling reminder that, while Yorkshire's industrial past is worth celebrating, much of what has been achieved is set against a background of sacrifice, shame and regret that children were 'put to the yoke' during the industrialisation of Britain. Time and again newspapers carried harrowing stories of disaster in the workplace, particularly in the mining industry. Poverty too has indiscriminately haunted the lives of working communities in both industrial and rural areas.

Hopefully, these times of adversity are now a thing of the past. Industry and commerce continue to move inexorably forward. Steam's supreme reign was eventually challenged in the twentieth century by electricity, instigating the dawn of 'Modern Britain' and a gradual transition to a cleaner, more efficient working environment.

Electricity is now at the heart of home and working life. Miniaturisation and 'instant access' to information and each other's lives have replaced the feeling of 'wonderment' with the word 'amazing'. It seems all the more relevant to view our current day achievements with a greater sense of historical perspective.

Recently, after being shown a video on the steel industry, which included a display of the impressive pyrotechnics involved in producing one of the world's largest castings, a group of Sheffield school children – after a brief moment of stunned silence – all rose as one, punched the air and cheered with youthful gusto. In paying tribute to Yorkshire's on-going craft skills and industrial achievements I would say that there are still a million reasons to shout a resounding 'Yes' to that.

TOP: *A reminder that throughout history, Yorkshire's impressive industrial legacy has not been achieved without a measure of tragedy and sacrifice.*

BELOW: *Iron and steel making continue to be a source of spectacular visual imagery. A 6,000 ton Davy forging press became the subject of a striking painting by artist, Brett Wagner.*

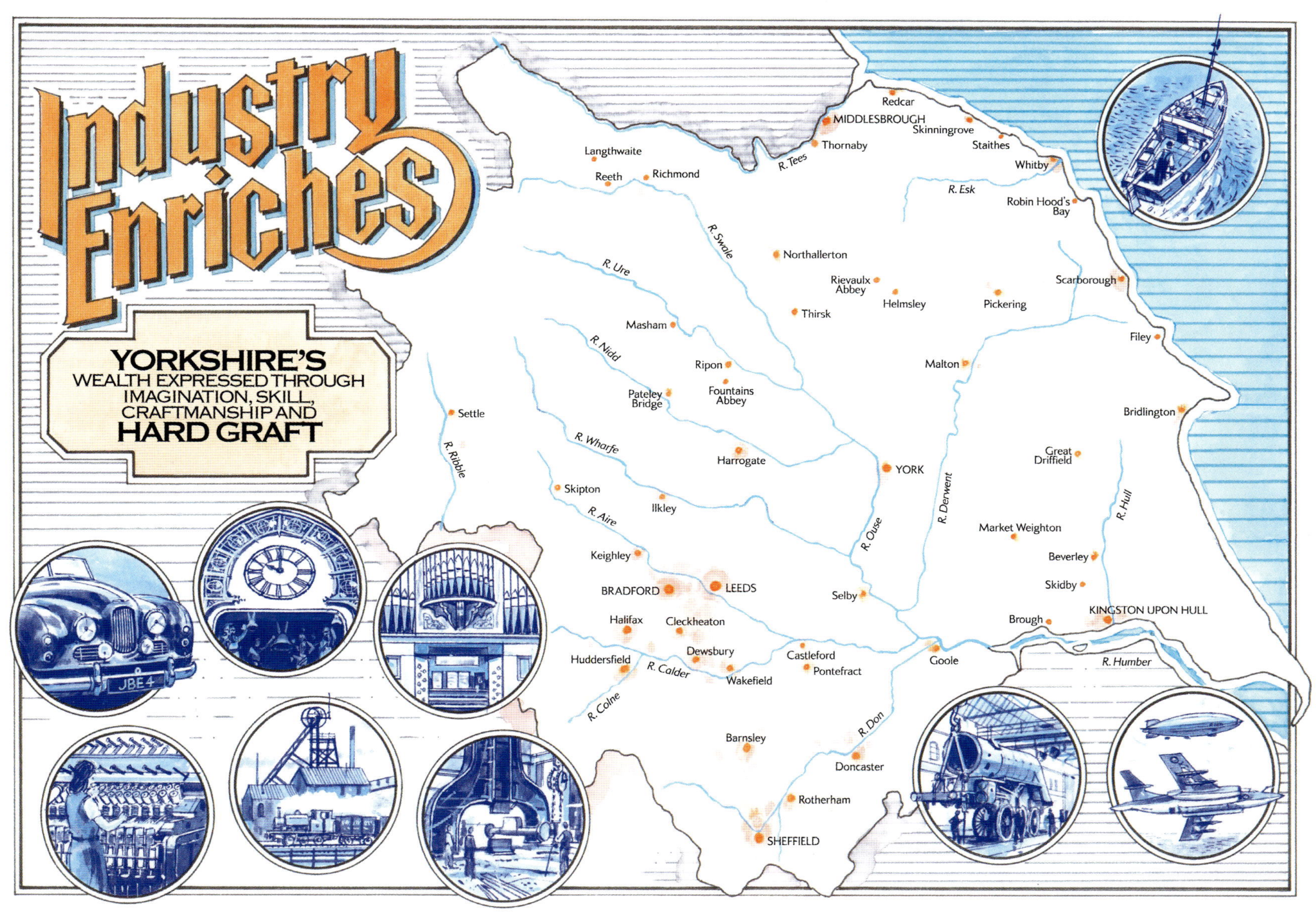

INDUSTRY ENRICHES: The insightful motto of the former Spenborough Urban District Council and Cleckheaton Secondary Modern School.

THE HAND OF GOD

The River Skell was turned into an all-important source of power by the monks who built Fountains Abbey. The present building dates largely from the early thirteenth century, the water mill was used to grind corn. After surviving the dissolution the mill continued to work until 1937. Recently restored, it is now regarded as one of the finest monastic mills in Europe.

The secluded, picturesque remains of Yorkshire's abbeys have always seemed a far cry from the county's crowded industrial heartland. But the apparent tranquillity and orderliness of monastic life belied the reality of an existence devoted not only to prayer and self denial but a great deal of hard graft and shrewd commercial acumen. The monastic centres of Fountains, Rievaulx, Byland, Kirkstall and others became early catalysts in establishing the foundations of industrial Yorkshire.

By the tenth century, monasteries in Europe had become wealthy institutions and were becoming increasingly immoderate. A rebellious group of Benedictine monks in France determined to return to St Benedict's original monastic principles of spiritual solitude, hard labour and frugality, founded the Cistercian Order. This more elementary ideology soon began to gain new converts and redefined monastic philosophy throughout Europe.

In 1132 the Cistercians established themselves at Rievaulx. Cistercian influence caused a small group of Benedictine monks at York to rebel. This insubordination brought about their expulsion, and in the depths of winter they found themselves living in caves on the banks of the River Skell, near Ripon. They eventually founded Fountains Abbey. A more lowly beginning to what would become one of the largest monastic settlements in Europe, cannot be imagined.

By the middle of the twelfth century the group's original timber church had been rebuilt in stone and had become part of a significant settlement. This pattern of expansion continued. Early Cistercian ideals were shed, as, by the thirteenth century, Fountains had become the largest and richest abbey of its Order in England.

Through a number of distant holdings and granges – the latter being outlying farms worked by monks or lay brothers – the estate covered large areas of Yorkshire, extending into parts of Cumberland and Lancashire. The wool from 15,000 sheep made the abbey a major player in Britain's most important industry at the time, with thriving export markets in Belgium and Italy being served through the ports of York and Boston.

The River Skell provided an important source of power to the water mill at Fountains. A mill has stood on this site since the twelfth century. Rebuilt and enlarged, it served as a corn mill and granary, and was probably used for other industrial purposes including sawing and fulling. Incredibly it survived as an operational mill until 1937.

Over thirty miles away in the Huddersfield area the monks of Fountains Abbey built a corn mill and iron forge at Bradley on the River Colne. The industrialisation of monastic life extended to the mining of lead and iron

ABOVE: The starkly beautiful remains of Fountains Abbey on the banks of the River Skell near Ripon. Founded by Cistercian monks in 1132, Fountains became one of the largest and most successful monastic settlements in Europe with landholdings from the River Tees in the north-east southwards to the River Calder.

LEFT: Stonemasonry on a much smaller, but no less grand a scale. Dating from about 1100, the Norman doorway at Healaugh St John, near Tadcaster, is a contemporary of Fountains Abbey, but pre-dates the Great West Door of York Minster by two centuries.

The hand of God. Twentieth century craftsmanship re-tells the first Bible story on the Great West Doorway of York Minster. Originally built around 1320, the ravages of time had taken their toll on the elaborate stonework, necessitating complete replacement. The newly carved doorway was unveiled in May 1998. The Genesis cycle is based on the designs of sculptor, Rory Young.

in Nidderdale, stone quarrying at a number of sites throughout Yorkshire, and a sizeable pottery at Winksley, a few miles north west of the abbey.

Henry VIII's break with Rome and his self appointment as Supreme Head of the church in England brought about the Dissolution of the Monasteries. These provided rich pickings for Henry's dwindling treasury. Fountains Abbey was sold to Sir Richard Gresham in 1540 and despoliation soon began. Stone, timber, lead and window glass were stripped and sold. Thankfully enough of the abbey survives today to provide a tangible link to four centuries of spiritual and industrial unity.

A finer appreciation of our great religious buildings can be realised by looking upwards, and taking the time to acknowledge and interpret the work of our forbears and their present day successors. Stonemasonry has manifest itself as one of the most powerful and enduring interpreters of past cultures. Wrought from the hard, uncompromising material from which our planet is made, the Great West Door of York Minster encapsulates this premise beautifully.

Originally carved in the fourteenth century, time and the elements had taken their toll on both the original and previous restoration work. In 1992 it was decided that renewal would be preferable to conservation. Examining past records enabled elements of the original design to be incorporated into the new work. Surrounded by ornate bands of stone depicting stylised foliage and animals and other creatures, the first biblical story is described in sixteen 'episodes'.

The narrative begins with God's creation of the universe; showing the hand of God holding planet earth emerging from the rays of the sun. Scenes from the book of Genesis follow; beginning with Adam and Eve in the Garden of Eden, through to Abraham's willingness to sacrifice his son Isaac to prove his faith in God.

This exquisite artistry has one more story to tell, and one more point to prove. The carving is crisp and sharp, with every form defined in proud relief. This is the work of twentieth century man, and a gratifying testament that we ourselves, – when put to it – are still able to create in the manner of our ancestors and aspire to desires other than those of commercial gain.

ABOVE: The original construction of York Minster is recalled in the timber scaffolding surrounding its west front. The stone yard can be seen in the foreground of this early twentieth century view.

INSET: Stained glass windows in our churches and cathedrals have imparted their own unique and colourful narratives to biblical and secular texts. The thirteenth century roundel shown is one of three depicting the seasons. Winter: shows a man about to kill a pig. Made by York glaziers, it can be seen in Dewsbury Minster.

ON THE EDGE OF A REVOLUTION

Built in the seventeenth century, the farmstead of Lower Blacup Farm near Cleckheaton, looked out onto mostly open fields and common land. Unlike some Yorkshire farms which have spent their entire lives in splendid isolation, Lower Blacup was destined to be close to significant, revolutionary events throughout the nineteenth century.

Like many farmsteads of the time, Lower Blacup had rooms set aside for the weaving of cloth on wooden handlooms. Before they could be sold the finished cloth 'pieces' were handed over to croppers; highly skilled cloth finishers who raised the surface (nap) on cloth with teasel spikes and then cropped it with large heavy iron shears to produce a smooth, even surface.

A blockade on Britain's ports during the Napoleonic war crippled the export trade vital to the cloth industry. Growing unemployment and high corn prices resulting from a succession of harsh winters brought the threat of starvation to many.

In 1809, William Cartwright who owned a mill about a mile away from Lower Blacup, installed a number of cropping frames. These were fairly crude devices that linked two pairs of cropping shears together enabling one man to do the work of ten.

Hosiery workers in the North Midlands began to sabotage knitting frames as their way of preserving jobs and livelihoods. The Luddite rebellion was born. In Yorkshire, mills harbouring the reviled cropping frames were attacked; culminating in a ferocious assault on Cartwright's mill in 1812. The mill building and its machinery were saved only by its owner's thorough preparation and the intervention of the military.

In 1839, at Peep Green, not far from Lower Blacup, an open air meeting organised by the Chartists to agitate for government reform attracted 250,000 people.

Discontent eventually turned to violence with insurgents attempting to close mills by drawing the fusible plugs of their boilers. In 1842 when rioters clashed with yeomanry called upon to defend St Peg Mills, Cleckheaton, the ensuing commotion may well have been heard at Lower Blacup.

Inevitably, once hostilities had died away, the mills became an accepted part of community life along with their supporting industries – ironfounding, engineering, mining and chemicals – changing the landscape of Cleckheaton and of Britain.

ABOVE: An isolated farm when first built in the seventeenth century, Lower Blacup, Cleckheaton, has, nevertheless, been within earshot of at least three well documented uprisings against mechanisation and government reform. The illustration shows Lower Blacup in the first decade of the twentieth century when industry had spread along the valley below, making workers in mills, mines, foundries and engineering workshops near neighbours of this once remote farmstead.

OPPOSITE PAGE: Rooms were set aside at Lower Blacup Farm for the weaving of cloth on wooden handlooms. The example shown has a jacquard attachment enabling patterns to be woven into the cloth.

RIGHT: Patented in 1787, the shearing or cropping frame became an object of hate to traditional hand croppers who were among the highest paid in the trade. The installation of cropping frames by early mill owners instigated the Luddite riots of 1812 in the Huddersfield area.

WEAVER TO WEARER

OPPOSITE PAGE: My great grandmother Eliza Ann Schofield and her friend pause briefly for their portraits beneath the flags and bunting decorating the weaving shed of a Bradford mill. The festive decorations celebrating the Diamond Jubilee of Queen Victoria in 1897 are in sharp contrast to the mechanical complexities of their weaving looms. Made by Bradford loom makers George Hodgson, they are typical of the thousands used in the textile industry. A weaving shed could contain up to fifty of these machines, instigating a racket that culminated in the relentless whip and crack of shuttles flying from one side of the machines to the other. Attending to a number of looms in her care would have been a truly intimidating experience to young girl at the start of her working life in the mill.

BELOW, LEFT: The power loom factory of George Hodgson Limited, Frizinghall, Bradford.

BELOW, RIGHT: Male operatives at Kaye and Stewart's mill, Huddersfield, stand beside their spinning frames made by Prince Smith of Keighley.

Water and later steam power, set in motion new forces in manufacturing. The workforce, many of them children, became part of a more relentless, more demanding environment. In the 1850s there were still hundreds of handloom weavers in Yorkshire, working in relative silence to the steadfastly measured wood-on-wood 'clack' of a shuttle. Metal would eventually win the day, but its unyielding durability did little for the art of conversation!

John Kay's flying shuttle of 1733, enabled weavers to speed up cloth production. Spinners eventually adopted the more efficient multi-spindled spinning jenny invented by James Hargreaves in 1764. Both significant developments, but still, at this time, rooted in the domestic system of cloth production.

The first steps towards the factory system were taken in the cotton industry in 1769 by a machine designed to be driven by something other than human muscle power. Richard Arkwright's water frame using rollers to draw the yarn could spin four threads at once. A horse provided the power in Arkwright's first spinning mill, but in 1771 he opened a water-powered cotton mill in Cromford, Derbyshire, creating a defining moment in our industrial history. Nine years later, using water-powered machinery operated under licence from Arkwright, Low Mill, Keighley, became Yorkshire's first cotton mill.

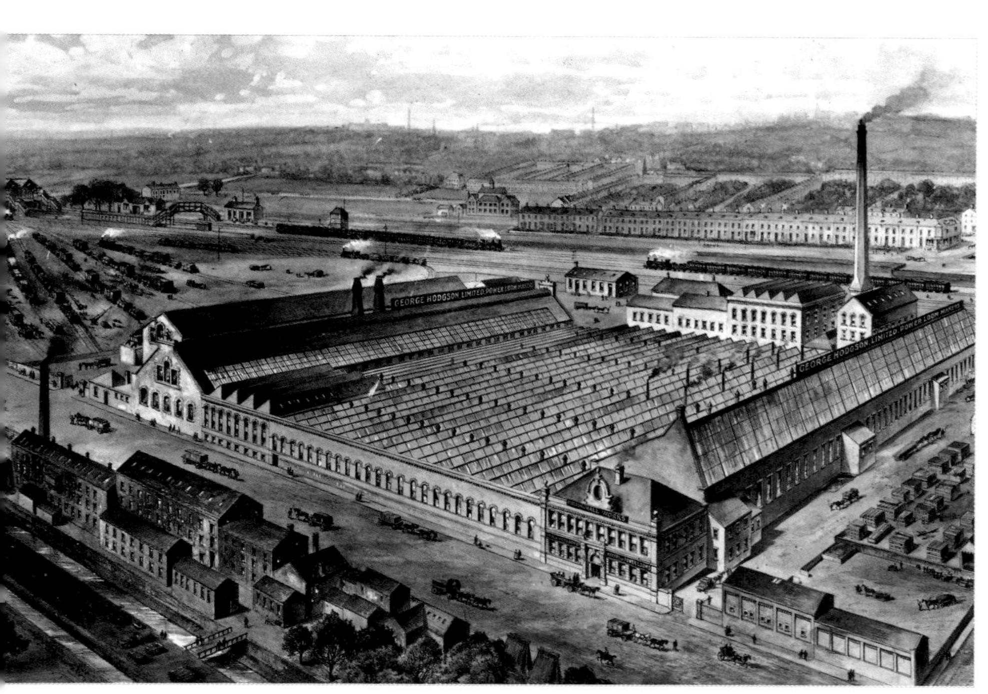

HODGSON
NOTICE

A weaver who spun his own yarn on an eight-spindled jenny, made the next significant advance in spinning. Samuel Crompton's mule of 1779 combined the best features of both jenny and water frame. Further development, including automation, enabled the mule to carry hundreds of spindles.

The power loom – a machine devised to match the significant strides made in spinning technology was invented by the Rev. Edmund Cartwright. His original application for a patent was done without any knowledge of handloom weaving! After several prototypes, the intricacies of the task were overcome, leading to Cartwright opening a cotton mill in Doncaster in 1786.

These inventions and others were further refined and developed by talented engineers – many of them Yorkshiremen – who contributed to the developing textile engineering industry's important role in the county's economic survival.

Engineering companies specialising in the production of all types of textile machinery sprang up in towns throughout Yorkshire. Keighley became a centre for both cotton and worsted production. But it was the town's textile engineering prowess that eventually put this Aire Valley town on the the world map.

In 1834 the first worsted power loom was designed and built in Keighley by George Hattersley. His father Richard had established himself as a machinist and whitesmith making bolts and screws, before moving on to spindles and rollers. Progress into power loom design and manufacturing under George's direction became the making of the company – now titled George Hattersley & Sons, Limited. For well over a century every aspect of power loom design and manufacturing was embraced by Hattersley's, whose machines could be found in cotton, wool, silk, and carpet manufacturing.

The accolades bestowed on Yorkshire's textile engineers were not confined to Hattersley's alone. Prince Smith & Company of Keighley, and George Hodgson Limited of Bradford, were just as highly regarded in the trade. All were regularly awarded gold medals at British and international exhibitions.

Unlike other machine makers, Hattersley's survived the decline of the textile industry in the 1960s, thanks to a modern version of the narrow fabric loom invented by them in 1908. Today, hot air balloons, polar husky dog teams and intercontinental haulage trucks use the straps and webbings made by Hattersley (Narrow Fabrics) Ltd.

OPPOSITE PAGE: At some stage between the sheep shearer and a tailor's skilfully wielded chalk and shears was this Hattersley power loom. Experience and intuition determined its mechanical complexity, enabling belts gears, cams and springs to work in well-oiled unison to produce the finest cloth. Built at the turn of the twentieth century by one of Keighley's premier textile machine makers, it is now preserved at the Bradford Industrial Museum.

BELOW, LEFT: Mechanics, or 'tuners', were responsible for keeping the machinery in mills in running order. A plain loom tuner stands beside a loom in the weaving shed at W.E. Jackson's Peel Mills, Morley.

BELOW, RIGHT: Like many of Yorkshire's textile towns, Keighley had more than one string to its bow. Five companies were producing domestic wringers, mangles and sewing machines; many were exported to all parts of the world from the town's railway station.

The invention of the sewing machine brought speedy mechanisation to the skilled but laborious task of hand stitching. At the Great Exhibition of 1851, Leeds tailor, John Barran witnessed an industrial bandsaw adapted to cut several layers of cloth at once. Using both machines, Barran opened a clothing factory in Leeds in 1856, thereby instigating one of Leeds' most successful industries; that of mass-produced clothing.

St Paul's House, Leeds, is one of the city's most striking landmarks. Faced in red brick with decorative Moorish minarets and tiles by Doulton, the word 'factory' doesn't readily spring to mind. The work of Thomas Ambler, this impressive building began life in 1878 as John Barran's second clothing factory, being equipped with machinery driven by gas engines and incorporating a hot water heating system.

John Barran went on to open an even larger clothing factory in Leeds; an inspiration no doubt to a Jewish refugee from Lithuania, who in 1910 also opened a factory in the city. In doing so Montague Burton began a clothing enterprise that would eventually eclipse that of his illustrious predecessor.

By setting up mechanised production lines and breaking down each process, Burton took the 'division of labour' and mass production in tailoring to new heights. Before the First World War he was producing made-to-measure gent's suits at twenty shillings – a price within the means of most working men at the time. By 1925, Montague Burton's latest clothing factory at Harehills, Leeds, had become the largest in Europe.

Dirt and grime from Britain's coal fired homes and industries were mantling buildings in our Victorian towns and cities. Into this sometimes decorative, but somewhat dour world, came gleaming white trailblazers of the 'new age' of jazz and streamlining – the cinemas. These oases of escapism adopted the very public face of Art Deco, a style originating from an exhibition of industrial and decorative art held in Paris in 1925 and rapidly embraced by the dream weavers of Hollywood.

Britain's Art Deco cinemas would have to share the spotlight with an equally new vision in retail tailoring. New from the ground-up, Montague Burton's shops with their Art Deco facades could be found throughout Britain, bringing prestige and style to the wardrobe of the British working man.

TOP: Moorish style minarets adorn St Paul's House, Park Square, Leeds. Designed by Thomas Ambler, this exotically styled building was originally a clothing factory owned by John Barran, one of the founders of the Leeds clothing industry.

LEFT: Of the many clothing manufacturers in the city, none was more successful than Montague Burton. An illustration from a catalogue of the 1950s reinforces Burton's 'Tailor of Taste' advertising slogan.

BELOW: The 'Black Prince', one of a fleet of distinctively styled streamlined delivery vans supplying Montague Burton shops from Truro to Aberdeen.

In 1932, a group of smoke begrimed Victorian shops on the corner of Princess Street and Old Market, Halifax, were replaced by a gleaming white vision of the future of retailing. Montague Burton's gents outfitters shop with its stylised Egyptian motifs, was the work of Burton's chief architect Harry Wilson, who used Art Deco – a style associated with the 'golden age of the cinema' – to give the name Montague Burton a recognisable and enduring presence in towns and cities throughout Britain.

The robust engineering required to harness the power of a major river like the Aire, is dramatically demonstrated by one of the two huge waterwheels at Thwaite Mills near Leeds. A mill has existed on this site for centuries. The present mill built in 1825, has, in more recent times, ground flint for the pottery industry, and chalk used in the manufacture of linseed oil putty. Thwaite Mills finally ceased commercial operations in 1976 and is now preserved as a working watermill.

POWER FOR A REVOLUTION

Centuries before the elements of fire and water were brought together to harness the expansive power of steam, the natural gravitational flow of rivers and streams was being bridled to provide a driving force beyond mere muscle power.

Early watermills were used primarily to grind corn. Windmills did not appear in the landscape until the twelfth century. The Domesday Survey of 1086 reveals that a hundred watermills were working in Yorkshire, serving manorial estates on which tenants were obliged to pay tolls or dues in kind to have their grain milled at the lord's mill.

Millwrights were among the first engineers. Like their contemporaries in boatbuilding, they worked initially in timber, iron not being widely available until the eighteenth century. With millstones weighing several hundredweights, transmitting the power behind a fast flowing river called for rugged mechanical components housed within sturdily constructed architecture.

The importance of this natural source of power to Britain's early

TOP: Lower Mill, Brighouse – one of the many corn and fulling mills on the River Calder. Dating back to 1518, the original fulling mill was subsequently rebuilt and enlarged. Lower Mill is shown in the latter half of the nineteenth century, when steam powered mills were dominating the town's skyline.

ABOVE: Fulling stocks in a Dewsbury mill on the River Calder. Built to pound or felt cloth, many working examples survived into the twentieth century.

The late George Watkins spent four decades from 1930, photographing Britain's stationary steam engines. Fortunately his camera also recorded a number of watermills and their machinery. This wonderfully atmospheric photograph taken in 1950, shows the water-driven tilt hammers, bar shears and grindstone at the edge tool forge of Tyzack & Turner's Little London Works, Sheffield.

industrial development cannot be overestimated. Water power was extensively used in fulling mills. 'Fulling' was part of the cloth finishing process, where cloth was washed and pounded by heavy hammers. This blended the fibres together, making the finished cloth much stronger – a seemingly over-engineered treatment of such an inherently flimsy material. It is easier to visualise this mechanical muscularity being applied to the processes of wood, chalk, stone and iron ore crushing.

In South Yorkshire, rivers like the Don and Sheaf unleashed their energy to realise Sheffield and Rotherham's industrial potential. Here, from the fifteenth century, scores of watermills were used by the early cutlery industry to drive furnace bellows and tilt hammers. In the lead mines of the Yorkshire Dales waterwheels were driving water pumps, ore crushing stamps and smelting furnace bellows.

The ruggedness of water powered machinery easily lent itself to crushing processes. In the pottery industry, flint was ground as an additive to glazes; ground chalk produced whiting for whitewash, putty and pharmaceuticals; exotic woods were crushed to produce dyes for the textile industry, and lubricants were made from crushed rape seed.

Millwrights working with both wind and water power had, thus far, benefitted from years of practical experience handed down from one generation to the next. By the eighteenth century engineering 'know-how' was being challenged by scientific theory, advocating that substantial progress could be achieved through greater efficiency.

John Smeaton, born in Whitkirk, near Leeds, in 1724, is chiefly remembered for his rebuilding of the Eddystone Lighthouse. Widely regarded as the father of civil engineering, Smeaton's early career began in the more miniature mechanical world of scientific instrument making. Windmills and watermills were a source of fascination to Smeaton who recognised a challenge in improving the efficiency of these important contributors to the local economy. To this end he built a number of models and submitted his findings to the Royal Society in 1759.

Smeaton's recommendations advanced the design and construction of watermills, recommending the use of iron for gears and shafting, and refinements in building and masonry work to maximise water flow. John Smeaton's improvements in watermill efficiency were vital in the transition from Britain's farm based existence to a factory based economy – a transformation felt none more so than in the textile industry.

Yorkshire's uplands with their attendant rivers and streams became the wellspring of an industry that would, in time, gain world renown. Wool, cotton, flax and silk were first spun and woven in relatively small mills. At

TOP: *The interior of the preserved Thwaite Mills, Stourton, Leeds, illustrates the uncompromising ruggedness of machinery driven by water power.*

ABOVE: *Water power was used in the lead industry for pumping water from mines and driving crushing machinery and furnace bellows. The photograph shows the 22ft diameter waterwheel driving crushing rollers at Old Providence Mills, Kettlewell, in Wharfedale.*

the beginning of the nineteenth century, out of the hundreds built, only a few were powered by steam.

Despite the construction of dams to improve the supply of water and the use of steam-powered beam engines as a means of pumping water back into the dams to maintain a supply, water-powered mills were always vulnerable to climactic extremes. Once steam power had got its foot in the door, the decline of water power was inevitable, but by no means swift. Well into the twentieth century there were still mills powered by a natural resource which gave birth to a world-wide revolution.

LEFT: The Fielden Brothers, cotton manufacturers of Todmorden built a 98-foot tower to house three waterwheels, one on top of the other at Lumbutts Mill. Three dams supplied water to the wheels, which, when working in unison could develop over fifty horse power for the adjacent cotton mill.

ABOVE: A single giant waterwheel provided the power to machinery at Foster Beck twine mill, Pateley Bridge, Nidderdale.

ABOVE: Water – the power that once drove the mule spinning frames at Staups Mill, still cascades down the narrow wooded valley between Hebden Bridge and Todmorden. Now a picturesque ruin, Staups Mill, built over two hundred years ago and owned initially by cotton manufacturer John Horsfall, was typical of the hundreds of Yorkshire mills built before the introduction of steam power.

LEFT: Aysgarth Falls, a familiar tourist attraction in Wensleydale where the River Ure once drove machinery at Yore Mill and a number of cotton mills situated along the dale.

THE SURVIVOR

Frank Meadow Sutcliffe's camera captures the five-sailed Union Mill, Whitby, a once prominent landmark in the town. Built in the first years of the nineteenth century it was run on co-operative lines by the Union Mill Provident Society Limited. In 1880 its sails and roof were severely damaged by a storm. Repaired, the mill continued until the disbanding of the Society in 1888.

A world away from its original, more pastoral environment, the rendered brick tower of Eyre's Mill stands firmly rooted in the car park of the Mill Inn in a bustling suburb of Hull, the sole survivor of ten corn mills which once lined Holderness Road. The fact that it exists at all is a minor miracle and must largely be due to having been owned by John Rank. He took possession of it in 1841, enabling the mill to play an important part in establishing the successful commercial reputation of one of Britain's premier corn and flour millers.

Out of the hundreds that have graced the landscape of our county since the first windmill was built at Weedley, East Yorkshire, by the Knights Templar in 1185, the mill at Skidby stands proudly on high ground between Beverley and Hull, as Yorkshire's lone working example. When restoration is complete Holgate Mill, York, will become the county's second working windmill.

Windmills could be found throughout Yorkshire, from the far north in locations like Pickering, Whitby, Kirkby Malham and Giggleswick, and the Pennine industrial towns of Golcar, Greetland, Keighley, Batley and Heckmondwike. Windmills were also operating in Sheffield, Rotherham, Hemsworth and Pontefract; areas that were later to become associated with mining and iron and steel making.

East of the Pennines, the more undulating landscape of the Yorkshire Wolds possessed the greatest concentration of windmills. It is said that here, in the East Riding, a windmill could be seen every six miles – a truly uplifting sight – especially on a clear day.

The earliest windmills were, in simple terms, a wooden shed or 'buck' atop a single massive upright baulk of timber – hence the name post mill. The body of the mill which carried the sails, millstones and gearing could be rotated on the post to face into or away from the wind. Yorkshire's last post mill at Little Smeaton near Pontefract endured a slow decline until its sudden disappearance in 1961.

All Yorkshire's surviving windmills are tower mills, which look like something resembling a lighthouse with sails. Built of brick or local stone, tower mills began to appear in significant numbers in the eighteenth century. Their more robust construction made them less vulnerable to storm damage and increased their operational versatility to include chalk

Having resolutely resisted the march of progress, Eyre's Mill defiantly rises from a car park of the Mill Inn in a busy
suburb of Hull. Though not now in working order, Eyre's Mill is the sole survivor of a number of corn mills that once
lined the Holderness Road. Dating from the eighteenth century the mill was, for a few years, owned by John Rank,
whose family established a reputation as one of the nation's leading flour millers.

LEFT: By 1934, Yorkshire's last remaining post mill looked like this. Hopes of preserving this unique windmill at Little Smeaton near Pontefract were dashed in 1961, when what remained of it suddenly disappeared overnight!

CENTRE: Preston's Mill, one of two windmills at Seaton Ross, a few miles west of Market Weighton, photographed in 1935 when it was still a working corn mill.

RIGHT: Windmills – a fascinating fusion of architecture and machinery. The sight and sound of timber, iron and stone working in unison can still be experienced by visitors to Skidby windmill which produces wholemeal flour from three sets of millstones.

crushing, oil seed crushing and flint grinding.

The great era of tower mill construction coincided with the gradual introduction of cast iron components into windmill machinery – an innovation attributed to John Smeaton's work to improve the efficiency of watermills. His experiments with models into the design of windmill sails led to the introduction of the more efficient five-sailed mill. The flint grinding tower mill built in around 1770 at the Leeds Pottery was a notable example.

A mill's productivity rested squarely on the shoulders of the miller and his skill in utilising every ounce of power from the prevailing winds. This involved keeping the sails facing into the wind – a skill known as 'winding'. Winding a post mill meant turning the body of the mill by hand on its central post and securing it with a 'spragg'. A miller caught with sails facing away from the wind (tail-winded) was in dire trouble and risked terminal damage to the mill's machinery. On a tower mill only the cap which included the sails could be turned. Many mills have what

ABOVE: A stirring sight for travellers journeying towards Hull and the Humber Bridge. Skidby windmill built in 1821was destined to become Yorkshire's last working windmill and now operates as an integral part of the Museum of East Riding Rural Life.

RIGHT: Windmills have been a source of inspiration to landscape artists and photographers for generations. Artist, Karl Wood (1888-1958) became almost obsessed by them. Travelling by bicycle, Wood set out to paint every windmill in Britain. His mission proved unsuccessful, but stands as one of the most comprehensive records to date. His painting of the derelict windmill at Swinefleet was completed in 1932.

The modern face of wind power. Wind turbines are part of Britain's aspirations to produce 'clean' electricity. Ovenden Moor Wind Farm near Halifax became operational in 1993. A landmark for miles around, its twenty three turbines produce sufficient electricity to power the domestic needs of over five thousand homes.

look like a miniature set of sails at the rear of the cap. This is the 'fantail' patented in 1745. The sails of the fantail are set at right angles to the main sails so that when the wind strikes it the main sails are automatically turned into the wind.

Main sails were at first a simple wooden framework with canvas attached by the miller every time he winded the mill. Their design progressed to give the miller greater control, for example, giving the sails a propeller-like pitch. The introduction of sails with spring loaded shutters to 'spill' the wind pressure of potentially damaging gusts led to a development which enabled the miller to regulate the opening and closing of the sail shutters in relation to wind speed. Invented by William Cubitt in 1807, this involved connecting the shutters by a rod and linking the sails at the centre by a system of cranks known as a 'spider'.

Despite progress in windmill design nature frequently had the last word. The wooden post mill at Wilberfoss was completely destroyed by a severe gale in 1838. Union Mill, Whitby, a stoutly built tower mill was severely damaged in a fierce storm. Flour milling creates a fine dust that can lead to an explosive chain reaction, resulting in devastation by fire.

For centuries windmills faithfully served the steady pace of a localised economy. In order to keep bread prices at an affordable level some mills were run by co-operatives and known as 'Union' or 'Subscription' mills. By the middle of the nineteenth century the surge in industrial and commercial activity had begun to re-define the parameters of supply and demand. The sight of a tall chimney adjacent to some windmills signified the use of a supplementary stationary steam engine, which meant that the miller was no longer totally reliant on the awe inspiring but fickle power of nature.

Out of a total of 171 corn mills in the East Riding in 1855 only 18 were operating by 1921. The very last – Skidby Mill – ceased using wind power commercially in 1954. The winds which once ground corn and crushed chalk, oil seed and flint now sweep across Yorkshire to produce electricity. Wind turbines – remote and untenanted – bring power to an on-line, flick-of-a-switch world. Like their predecessors they are landmarks of their time.

LABYRINTH BENEATH THE LANDSCAPE

TOP: Lead mining in the Yorkshire Dales goes back centuries. Opened in 1790 and closed in 1898, the remains of the smelt mill at Old Gang Mine in the valley of Hard Level Gill, Swaledale, are a tangible reminder of a prolific industry that was once a world leader.

BELOW: Ten miles north of Whitby and close to some of Yorkshire's highest sea cliffs, is Boulby Potash Mine, first opened in 1973 in an area once noted for alum and ironstone. Boulby supplies a growing demand for fertilizer and salt for road de-icing. Shafts up to 1500 metres deep enable scientists based at the mine to carry out experiments into cosmic rays in the quest to unravel the secret of dark matter.

In the 1950s – the days of my childhood – I can remember playing on huge mountains of grey shale that rose thirty feet or more from some of the surrounding fields. In the shadow of one of these man-made hills was a brick structure, ten or fifteen feet high and devoid of doors windows or roof.

Youthful exuberance, mixed with a modicum of mischief, discovered that, by lobbing a stone over the rim, its descent into the abyss could be timed – one…two…three…four…until a distant echoing thump signalled the missile's abrupt arrival into an unknown, black mysterious world beneath our feet.

This simple edifice and its attendant 'pit-hill' were the last visible remains of Highmoor Lane Pit, Cleckheaton, once one of a number of small privately owned coal mines in the area, some of which were owned by the famous Low Moor Iron Works.

By the 1930s, the coal and ironstone seams worked by these mines had been exhausted, bringing closure, demolition and clearance; but leaving a substantial subterranean network of abandoned, now largely forgotten, passageways and tunnels.

Working the land and exploiting the mineral resources beneath have co-existed since the Bronze and Iron Ages, when our forbears let the natural forces of wind, rain and ice rip and scour the topsoil to expose any mineral deposits beneath. The Romans used this method to excavate ironstone, lead and coal directly from where it outcropped at the surface.

After the Norman Conquest, land and its mineral rights were divided between Lords of the Manor and the monastic houses. By the thirteenth century, small scale mining activity was being carried on throughout Yorkshire.

Miners began sinking shallow vertical shafts and working outwards as far as it was safely possible, creating what were known as bell-pits. Mining by drift or adit – which meant tunnelling directly into a hillside or outcrop – was practised in coal, ironstone and lead mining. For centuries, basic tools and candlelight were the only means to make headway.

Landowners commissioned surveys in the hope of finding a fortune in 'black gold' beneath their wheat crops and grazing cattle. The Sisters pit in the Garforth area on the outskirts of Leeds was opened in 1843, being one of a group of collieries on land owned by the Gascoigne Family of Parlington Hall. Surrounded by prime agricultural land the pits were named after the daughters of the owner of the estate and were linked by the privately owned Aberford Railway which made a connection with the Leeds & Selby Railway opened in 1834. This enabled the coal produced, to find a wider market. The locomotive illustrated was made by Manning Wardle of Leeds and is typical of those built for colliery and industrial use.

In Swaledale and Arkengarthdale, lead miners adopted a technique known as 'Hushing', where water courses were damned and then breached allowing the resulting torrent to expose ore bearing veins.

By the nineteenth century Britain had become the world leader in lead production. In Yorkshire it was centred around Swaledale, Arkengarthdale and Grassington Moor. Below ground a complex system of shafts and levels; above, the moors would be swathed in smoke from smelt mills where the crushed ore or galena was extracted by being melted in a furnace.

Lead mining in the Dales survived a number of slumps in the industry, but its terminal decline by the end of the nineteenth century meant that mechanisation never fully made an impact.

Ironstone mines were worked in Rosedale on the North York Moors in medieval times. But it was not until the middle of the nineteenth century that this remote part of Yorkshire was transformed into a bustling industrial landscape. The West Mines near Rosedale Abbey were opened in 1856 to be followed by others and the establishment of a sizeable community. By opening a branch line with a direct connection to Middlesbrough, the North Eastern Railway provided a lifeline to the mines, enabling them to survive isolation and harsh winters until mining ceased in 1926.

Ironstone mining came to Yorkshire's north east coast in 1848 with the opening of mines at Skinningrove near Loftus, an area previously noted for alum and sandstone, although ironstone nodules had been harvested from the foreshore for some time. Ironstone seams running inland were exploited by drift mining, meeting with enough success to justify the establishment of the Skinningrove Iron Company Limited. The ironstone mines endured the peaks and troughs common throughout the mining industry. Many closed, only to briefly re-open again. Sadly, all had gone by the time the Loftus mine closed in 1958.

The Yorkshire Coalfield stretches from Leeds, Bradford and Halifax at its northerly edge, to Sheffield, Doncaster and beyond in the south of the county. Without coal and its by-product coke, industries like iron and steel, glass, pottery, brick-making, textiles, chemicals, shipping and the railways, would have struggled to progress or even exist.

Although originally promoted by Yorkshire wool merchants, the coal industry was to benefit greatly from the opening of the Aire & Calder Navigation in 1702. This marked the first stage in the construction of Yorkshire's inland waterway system that would bear the burden of bulk transport until the rapid growth of the railways during the nineteenth century.

OPPOSITE PAGE, TOP: *The monks of Fountains Abbey first exploited the lead veins on Grassington Moor in the fifteenth century. For three hundred years mining was done by bell pits and shallow shafts, until the Duke of Devonshire provided the capital to reach deeper, richer veins in the early nineteenth century. In what is now one of Yorkshire's most popular tourist areas, it is now almost impossible to imagine an industrial complex on the scale of Old Moss Lead Mine, The mine was at its most productive during the nineteenth century, before mining activity ceased on Grassington Moor in the 1880s.*

OPPOSITE PAGE, BELOW: *In drift mining (one of the earliest mining methods), miners worked directly into a hillside or outcrop. This practice was favoured in both lead and ironstone mining. Illustrated, is the drift entrance to the ironstone mine at East Mines in Rosedale, North Yorkshire. Opened in 1860 the operation closed with the rest of the mines in 1926.*

ABOVE: *'There was no lovelier place on earth'. A quote from a local newspaper, decrying the despoliation of the natural beauty of a wooded valley at Skinningrove, North Yorkshire, in order to supply the insatiable need for iron in the nineteenth century. The Loftus Ironstone Mines commenced mining in Skinningrove in 1848. The photograph dates from 1903, by which time offices, workshops, stables, cottages and railway sidings had been built. Steam issues from the compressor house powering giant fans providing ventilation to the mines. Above the valley, to the left, just out of the picture, was further industrialisation in the shape of the Skinningrove Ironworks.*

The first railways were built specifically to carry coal. The introduction of the steam locomotive enabled coal to be moved in vast quantities to an ever widening market.

Decades before the railways, mining was the first industry to harness the power of steam to pump water from flooded seams, and as shafts went ever deeper, steam engines powered pit-head gear and ventilation equipment.

In the past the Yorkshire Coalfield has supported hundreds of mines ranging from small collieries, some quite close to town centres, to more isolated deep mines like Brodsworth Main, north of Doncaster. Brodsworth became the largest deep mine in the county, its deepest shaft reaching 839 yards. Here in 1957, three thousand six hundred men produced a record breaking 34, 422 tons of coal in one week.

Coal seams vary in size and thickness, from the 600 square miles and up to 900 yards deep Barnsley Bed, to smaller seams like the quaintly named Pot Clay Seam, probably no more than three feet in thickness and used in the manufacture of clay pipes.

To the layman one lump of coal may look very much like another, but coal seams have specific qualities, making them suitable for coking, gas, steam raising and domestic use.

Always the most physically demanding of jobs, mining has throughout its existence relied on hand tools and muscle power. Only during the early part of the twentieth century did mechanisation begin to make a significant impact below ground with the introduction of compressed air coal cutters and drills, and the early use of coal-carrying conveyor belts. In 1939 the Hunslet Engine Company, Leeds, built Britain's first flameproof diesel locomotive for working underground.

Although in more recent times electricity has supplanted steam power and powerful hydraulic shearers now slice effortlessly into coal faces, mining is still reliant on human skill and effort to maintain mastery of that dark labyrinth beneath the landscape.

TOP: The simple bucket-like device in the centre of the picture is a kibble. The heavy-duty chain it hangs by must have been a reassuring sight to the men lowered and raised hundreds of feet during pit sinking operations. The kibble at Bullcroft Colliery near Doncaster is full to capacity for the benefit of the photographer recording the scene in 1912.

ABOVE: Hard graft. Cramped conditions for both miner and photographer. Jeff Poar's superb study shows Reuben Kenworthy working the sixteen-inch high Beeston Seam at Emley Moor Colliery near Huddersfield.

Disc coal-cutters were among the first examples of mechanisation underground in coal mining. The deep undercut disc coal-cutter illustrated was made by the Diamond Coal Cutter Company of Normanton in 1898. Compressed air provided a safe source of power in a potentially hazardous working environment.

In 1924, Doncaster photographer, E.L. Scrivens captured the atmosphere of a working colliery with this fine photograph of Frickley Colliery, South Elmsall. First sunk in 1903, Frickley was, like many other collieries, equipped with workshops for general maintenance, blacksmithing and wagon repairs. The complex also included a brickworks and a power station. The latter produced compressed air and supplied electricity to local villages and the National Grid.

Collieries have so often nurtured social and recreational facilities, Frickley was no exception, supporting athletics, football and boxing clubs, and of course, the well known Frickley Colliery Brass Band.

Throughout its life, Frickley underwent continual modernisation. Coal production hit a yearly target of 1,000,000 tons in 1956. Eventually production costs began to outweigh profitability, leading to closure in 1993 with the loss of 740 jobs. Frickley became yet another casualty of the once mighty Yorkshire Coalfield.

OPPOSITE PAGE, TOP: The residents of a housing estate in Durkar on the outskirts of Wakefield had a coal mine as a very near neighbour. Privately owned and displaying a quirkiness that could only be found in a small-scale operation, Bramwyn No1 Colliery – or Peggy Tub Main, as it was known locally – was one of Yorkshire's smallest mines. It closed in 1951.

OPPOSITE PAGE, BELOW: The first section of the Aire & Calder Navigation was opened in 1704. The canal continues to be a viable working element in this twenty-first century industrial landscape. The strikingly white architecture of Kellingley Colliery near Knottingley is framed by power lines and lofty pylons and the distant backdrop of Ferrybridge Power Station – symbols of the nation's dependence on electricity generation and the natural resource of coal.

BEHIND THE BANNER

Described by *The Illustrated London News* as 'A very dreadful explosion', the blast that ripped through Oaks Colliery near Barnsley claimed the lives of 73 miners. Traumatised relatives rushed anxiously to the scene that Saturday afternoon in 1847. Sadly, such terrible events in the mining industry were not an uncommon occurrence.

In mining and elsewhere, children were expected to work to help their families 'make ends meet'. Almost a decade before the Oaks disaster, 26 children between the ages of 7 and 17 were drowned when a violent thunderstorm sent a torrent of water into coal seams at Husker pit, Silkstone. An Act passed in 1842 prohibiting the employment of females and boys under the age of ten in mines would have spared 26 lives at Husker.

Tragedy struck again at Oaks Colliery in December 1866, when two explosions killed 361 men and boys. The appalling death toll made it England's worst mining disaster, and included the names of 26 men who went to the rescue of their fellow miners.

The names of Oaks and Husker are but two on a roll-call that includes Cadeby, Lundhill, Morley, Thornhill, Darley Main Swaith Main and Bentley. Here, and in many other places are memorials to remind us that misfortune has continually stalked those engaged in bringing coal and ore from deep beneath our planet's more familiar outer skin.

Sadly too, history has not left unrecorded times of recession when poverty came swiftly over the threshold of every family; the shockwave rippling outwards to impair the livelihood's of neighbouring shopkeepers and traders.

Danger and hardship have combined to nurture a community with a bond like few others. Healing and revival being aided by a collective sense of humour and competitive camaraderie expressed through sport, horticulture and music.

At the National Union of Mineworkers offices in Barnsley, union branch banners hang in the Miners' Hall. On gala days, miners, officials and their families march through crowded streets 'behind the banner' preceded by a colliery brass band, reaffirming the bond that binds our mining communities.

ABOVE: A national strike by miners in 1912 to secure a minimum wage lasted for six weeks. With the pits closed, outcropping for coal became a familiar sight throughout the Yorkshire Coalfield. Miners and their families 'pull together' in Warren Quarry Lane, Barnsley.

OPPOSITE PAGE TOP: The Illustrated London News *depicted distraught relatives and friends gathering at the scene of England's worst mining disaster. On the 12th of December 1866 two explosions rocked Oaks Colliery, Barnsley, claiming the lives of 361 miners. An explosion at the mine in 1847 killed 73 men.*

OPPOSITE PAGE BELOW: A photograph from happier times. In the foreground, members of the Brodsworth Main branch of the NUM proudly carry their banner along Bennetthorpe, Doncaster, during a miners' gala in the early 1960s.

THE POWER TO CHANGE

Water has forever been the scourge of the mining industry. As shafts grew deeper pumps worked by men or horses proved barely adequate. In 1698, Devonian, Thomas Savery, patented a 'fire machine for drawing water from mines'. This used the vacuum created, when steam in an enclosed vessel is condensed, to lift water from flooded mine workings. With no moving parts, Savery's device was little more than a fairly elaborate pump; but it provided a valid prologue to the opening chapter of the story of steam power.

In 1712, a century before the Middleton Colliery railway, Leeds, became the first in the world to use steam locomotives, coal seams at Tipton in the Staffordshire coalfield were being pumped dry by a machine that would be the true forerunner of things to come.

Thomas Newcomen, an ironmonger from Dartmouth, Devon, built the revolutionary 'atmospheric engine' that kept Tipton's rising flood waters at bay. A piston in a vertical cylinder, open ended at the top, was connected to a massive overhead beam centrally pivoted on an outside wall of the engine house. Steam admitted to the underside of the piston was condensed by a spray of cold water, creating a vacuum. Atmospheric pressure above the piston created the power stroke forcing the beam downwards, lifting the pump rods connected to its opposite end. Cooling the cylinder at the end of each stroke meant that early Newcomen engines were prodigious users of coal. Other engineers including John Smeaton sought to develop and refine the steam engine during its early rise to industrial greatness.

Scottish engineer James Watt significantly improved the efficiency of Newcomen's engine by incorporating a permanently hot cylinder and separate condenser. This eliminated the wasteful process of heating and cooling earlier beam engine cylinders.

These early developments in stationary steam paved the way for the tens of thousands built and maintained with skill and care to work for decades in every facet of industry.

Yorkshire's first cotton mill, Low Mill, Keighley (1780), became the first in the county to use a beam engine to pump water back into the dam. This maintained the flow of water to its water wheel – a practice taken up by other mills.

J.B.CLABOUR
GUISELEY YORKS

A photograph that illustrates both the scale and superb workmanship found in stationary steam engines. This example was originally built by Bowling Ironworks, Bradford, in 1870, as a twin compound beam engine for John Priestman & Company, Ashfield Mills, Thornton, near Bradford. It was later modified by Woodhouse & Mitchell of Brighouse, to increase its power output from 60 to 100hp. This magnificent machine ran until the 1950s when it was scrapped in favour of a diesel generating plant and electric motor drives.

Britain's industrial development was gaining momentum; but to enable steam power to drive machinery, a rotary motion had to be devised. Around 1780, the crank and flywheel – one of steam engineering's fundamental principles – was born. The invention of the rotative beam engine has been attributed to a number of engineers working on the idea at the same time, not least of which was James Watt, who joined forces with Matthew Boulton to form Boulton & Watt. As Britain's leading builder of stationary steam engines at that time they supplied engines to Yorkshire textile mills. However, this legendary company soon found itself competing against local iron founders such as Emmett's of Birkenshaw near Leeds, Bowling Iron Works, Bradford, and Fenton Murray & Wood of Leeds who were building steam engines for local industry.

In the first decades of the nineteenth century steam became a power in its own right. Mills were no longer reliant on the vagaries of a water supply and could be built anywhere.

Beam engines continued to be built well into the nineteenth century. The introduction of machine tools capable of working to thousandths of an inch brought technical advancement and precision to workshop practice. Beam engines, once robustly, if not crudely made were now examples of engineering excellence.

In the 1850s the rotative principle became the basis of other types which did away with the beam altogether. Of these, the two most significant were; the vertical steam engine, in which the cylinder(s) were positioned above the crankshaft and flywheel, and the horizontal engine with its cylinder(s), flywheel and crankshaft arranged in a horizontal plane. This variant became the most widely used of all stationary steam engine types.

Across Yorkshire's industrial heartland engineering companies were taking up the challenge to supply steam power to the county's flourishing industries.

A few miles west of Halifax in the Calder Valley – where mills once lined the river and canal banks – is Sowerby Bridge. Fronting on to the town's main street was Bank Foundry, founded in 1786 by Timothy Batesa manufacturer of beam engines. A generation later the firm passed on to Joseph Pollit, a relative of Bates, who, in 1865 was joined by marine engineer, Eustace Wigzell. Together they went on to become one of Britain's leading marine and stationary steam engine builders – Pollit & Wigzell – exporting to countries throughout the world. Sowerby Bridge was also the home of Wood Bros., another important name in steam engine building.

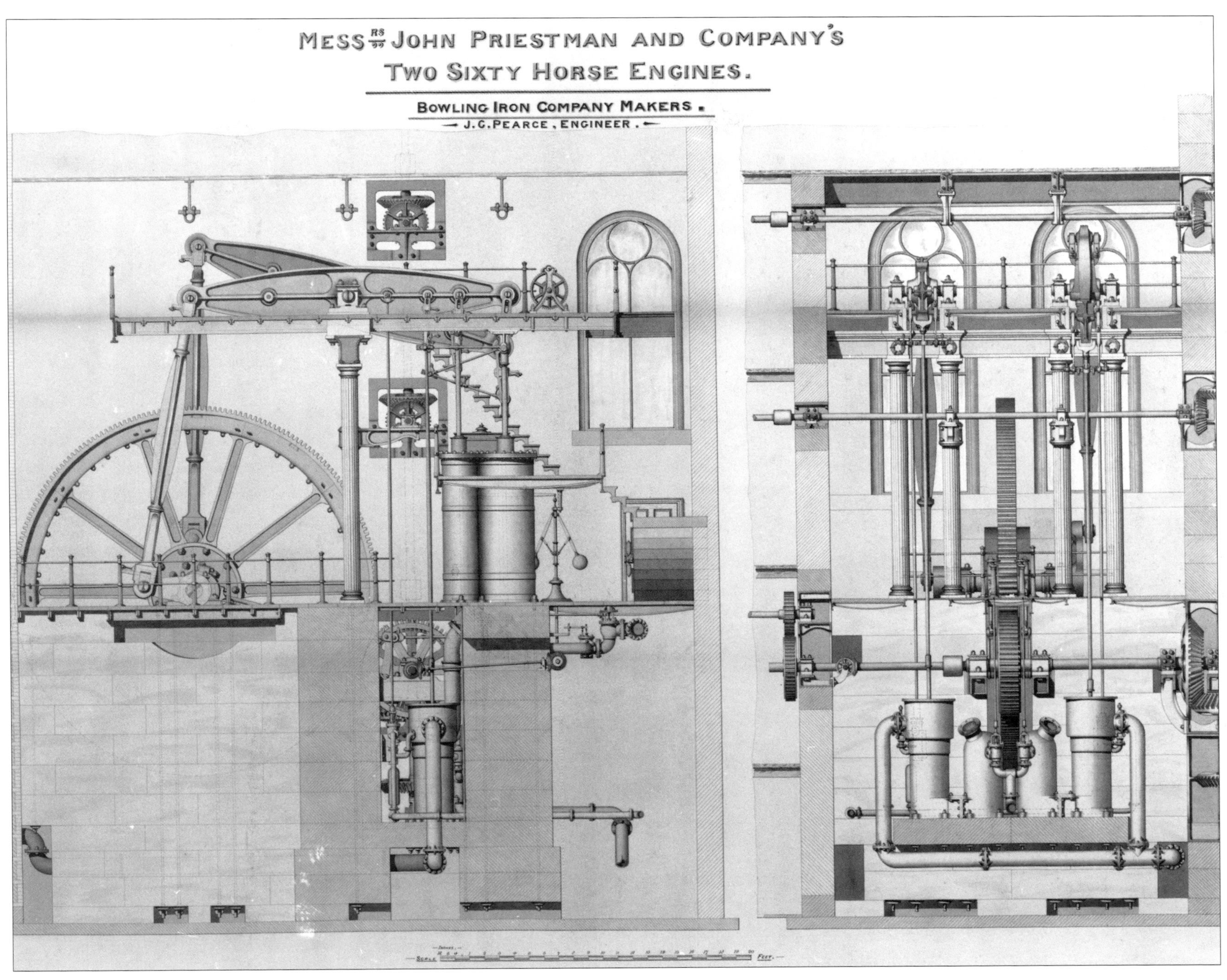

A beautifully rendered line and wash drawing of the Bowling Ironworks beam engine shown in the photograph on the opposite page. The drawing office was an important area of the manufacturing process. Before the introduction of computer aided design, draughtsmen working with traditional drawing instruments produced a multitude of detailed drawings from which those on the shop floor could work.

Other companies like Cole, Marchant & Morley, founded by two former employees of Bowling Iron Works, and Newton, Bean & Mitchell, both of Bradford, became leading builders, as did Bradley & Craven, Wakefield; Marsden's Engines, Heckmondwike; Woodhouse & Mitchell, Brighouse and Davy Bros. of Sheffield. Some companies produced hundreds of steam engines, others were to make only a handful. Cole, Booth & Porter are known to have built only three.

Engine builders were committed to getting the most out of every pound of steam. Power output could be increased through 'compounding' in which high-pressure steam was re-used in a low-pressure cylinder. Depending upon the application, engines ranged from 10hp to 12,000hp – a figure achieved by the three-cylinder vertical steam engine built by Davy Bros. in 1905 for Cammell's armour plate rolling mill in Sheffield.

Few people working in a textile mill would set foot inside the firm's engine house – an inner sanctuary, where order and cleanliness reflected the high regard for craftsmanship and mechanical perfection. Efficiency was masterfully managed as the engine relentlessly performed its task with not a wisp of wasted steam. Pride in the job must have enabled an engine built by Carr, Foster & Co. of Bingley to work for 120 hours a week for over 70 years – a feat not unknown in this sphere of engineering. Longevity was built into stationary steam engines, but it failed to prevent the inevitable all-conquering take-over by electricity.

Today, people go out of their way to see the sight of a steam locomotive in full cry; the epitome of the living, breathing, power of steam – a romantic evocation of journeys past or experiences that might have been.

Stationary steam engines have served us in a completely different way, being the hidden and unsung driving force behind just about every industrial process. Their contribution to Britain's past reputation as 'the workshop of the world' deserves to be more widely acknowledged.

BELOW, LEFT: Typical of the hundreds of steam engines found throughout Yorkshire, this 250hp Pollit & Wigzell horizontal tandem steam engine worked alongside an older beam engine at Whitworth & Co., Cooperhouse Mills, Luddendenfoot, near Halifax.

BELOW, RIGHT: Despite their size and power, stationary steam engines were designed to be subservient to their masters. This clock-like mechanism on a 1000 hp Pollit & Wigzell engine enables the governor (a device for maintaining a constant speed) to be finely regulated.

Originally built around 1830, the torched eye-less window sockets of New Bank Mill stare blankly out over the town centre of Halifax.
Built for George Haigh & Sons, cotton & worsted spinners, New Bank was one of Halifax's early steam powered mills.
The long narrow window on the right-hand side identifies this as the engine house which would have been the location of a beam engine.
The illustration dates from the 1990s. A listed grade II building, the mill miraculously survived to undergo conversion into apartments.

COTTAGE KITCHEN TO KING'S TABLE

TOP: Creamware was just one of the many wares produced by the Leeds Pottery in the Hunslet area of the city. This delicate cruet with its pierced decoration would have been made within earshot of Leeds' many railway engineering foundries.

BELOW: A number of Yorkshire brickmakers produced items of pottery in limited numbers. William Ingham established a firebrick works in Wortley, Leeds, in 1825. In the 1880s, before its eventual amalgamation with the Leeds Fireclay Company, Ingham's made a small quantity of vases, figures and statues.

In the early part of the nineteenth century, a kestrel hovering over Hunslet moor on the southern fringes of Leeds, would be looking down on a changing landscape. The city, like many others, had begun to embrace commerce, manufacturing and mass production. Steam was beginning to supplant wind and water power, accelerating the industrial growth that would sweep away acres of fields and hedgerows.

The kestrel may have picked up thermal currents from the distinctively bottle-shaped kilns of the Leeds Pottery, founded in 1770 by Richard Humble and John and Joshua Green.

Leeds Pottery was Yorkshire's largest factory pottery. A five-sailed flint grinding windmill dominated the south-eastern corner of the site, although this process was transferred to a water-powered mill at Thorpe Arch near Wetherby. This in turn was superseded by the installation of a stationary steam engine at Leeds Pottery in the 1830s. The pottery complex in common with other factory potteries, included a number of kilns, clay yards, drying house, slip house, carpenters, blacksmiths and general workshops, offices and stables.

Local clay was used to make a wide variety of domestic wares; but Leeds Pottery is now remembered for its white bodied creamware. Made from fine Cornish clays it is more widely known as 'Leedsware' and is highly valued by collectors.

The origins of pottery go well beyond Yorkshire's boundaries in both distance and time. But there is in this particular industrial landscape, a world 'first'. The steam locomotive with its rake of coal-filled chaldron wagons is running on Charles Brandling's colliery railway, built as a horse drawn wagon-way in 1758 to transport coal from his mines in Middleton to the River Aire in the centre of Leeds. In 1812, Brandling and his colliery manager John Blenkinsop inaugurated the world's first commercially successful steam powered railway.

Coal and the fireclay found with it were of paramount importance determining the geographic affiliation between the pottery, mining, brick and glassmaking industries. The majority of Yorkshire potteries – there were over a hundred by the nineteenth century – were situated near the

A birds-eye view of Leeds Pottery, when the Hunslet district of south Leeds was largely open fields and moorland.
Founded in 1770, Leeds Pottery, Yorkshire's largest factory pottery, became noted for its earthenware or 'Leedsware'. In
the middle distance can be seen the tower of a once five-sailed flint mill and, beside it stands the chimney serving its
eventual successor, a stationary steam engine. After several ownerships, the pottery closed in 1888.
Running through the pottery yard is a steam locomotive hauling wagons of coal on the Middleton Colliery railway,
which, in 1812 became the world's first commercially successful line to use steam haulage. In 1960 the Middleton
Railway Preservation Society led the way in the British railway preservation movement.

county's major coalfields – an exception being a small isolated coalfield serving a group of potteries at Burton in Lonsdale, near Ingleton.

Navigable rivers and canals serving the mining industry before the coming of the railways provided potteries with the means to export finished wares, and import clay from areas like the West Country to produce quality fineware.

Pottery, a craft that has defined the cultural advancement of successive civilisations, has been practiced in Yorkshire for centuries. Early potters, scattered throughout the county, worked single-handedly, or as small family units using local clay to produce domestic wares for their immediate neighbourhood. In this respect, a typical cluster of early potteries could be found at Potovens, an area now known as Wrenthorpe, near Wakefield.

The latter half of the eighteenth century became the genesis of Britain's industrial revolution. A burgeoning population and increased demand began to overwhelm craft-based enterprises. Pottery moved into mass-production and the business world of investors and entrepreneurs gradually took away the livelihoods of scores of small family-run concerns.

In 1785, Leeds Pottery amalgamated with Swinton Pottery, another of Yorkshire's great factory potteries, in a partnership that lasted for twenty one years – a respectable achievement in an industry plagued by bankruptcies, and regular changes of ownership. Both management and workforce were apt to move from pottery to pottery.

At their peak, factory potteries were major employers. An advertisement from 1835, relating to the sale of the Don Pottery between Swinton and Mexborough, makes reference to the company's 600 employees.

Jugs, bowls, jars and bottles, the earthenware chattels of everyday life were produced in vast quantities by Yorkshire's factory potteries. In complete contrast, many of these companies were making finewares and artwares to compete with the best from Staffordshire, Devonport, and Worcester. Pattern books stimulated the home market and established export trading with Europe, Russia, North and South America and Australia.

Art potteries, alluding to 'true artistic principles' came into being. With a workforce of almost a hundred, Linthorpe Art Pottery, Middlesbrough, produced wares where applied ornamentation was subservient to the purity of line. Closed in 1889 after trading for only ten years, several Linthorpe employees moved to Burmantofts Pottery, Leeds, whose art and faience pottery was of a much more florid nature.

After gaining the patronage of William IV in 1830, Swinton Pottery was able to use the mark 'Brameld. Royal Rockingham Works. Manufacturers to the King', ensuring that their fine Rockingham porcelain graced the dining tables of England's great houses.

Wares from Leeds, Castleford Mere – famous for the work of David Dunderdale – Ferrybridge, Swinton, the Don Pottery and the products from Middlesbrough and Hull, are highly valued by private and museum collections throughout the world.

Yorkshire's factory potteries have long since gone, but throughout the county independent potters and potteries continue to bring fresh insight and inspiration to this most ancient of crafts.

OPPOSITE PAGE: 1. One of the 'chattels of everyday life' – a survivor from a long-forgotten pantry or cellar. This unmarked stoneware egg jar (now minus its lid) could have been made by almost any Yorkshire pottery in the nineteenth century.

2. Treasured and highly valued. Rockingham porcelain, made in Swinton, South Yorkshire between 1830 and 1842, found favour with the highest echelons of society. The tray illustrated depicts a painting of Denton Park, South Yorkshire.

3. Deep, rich colour allied to a purity of line influenced by Oriental wares. An earthenware vase from the 1880s is typical of the work of the Linthorpe Art Pottery, Middlesbrough, the first pottery in Britain to use gas fired kilns.

4. 'MY DAUGHTER, Pleased with her Doll as Child could be, Who did with sweet alacrity, Put Doll to Bed and work with me, MY DAUGHTER': Creamware plate by Ferrybridge Pottery.

5. Burmantofts Pottery & Wilcock and Co. (Leeds) 1882-1904: A striking tin-glazed earthenware wall plaque from one of Yorkshire's art potteries.

6. Once commonplace, but now extremely rare: A slipware knife box dated 1858, by Howcans Pottery, Northowram, Halifax; a small pottery that also made firebricks and chimney pots.

7. Small, independent potteries continue to thrive in Yorkshire: A charming slipware money box by Peter Dick of Coxwold Pottery, near Ampleforth.

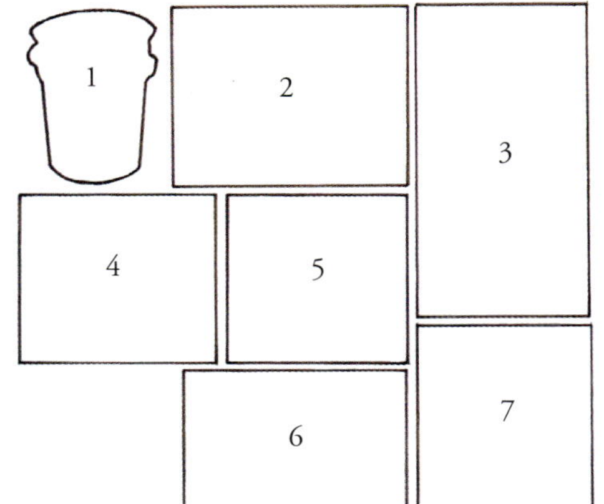

1812 OVERTURE: THE START OF A WORLDWIDE INDUSTRY

The year is 1910, and a snow covered mountain pass in the South American Argentine Andes echoes to the sound of a steam locomotive blasting its way up a single track railway line.

In true mountain-railway style, the engine is using the rack principle, where a toothed rail between the track engages with a cog on the locomotive, providing extra grip as it hauls its train up formidable inclines to the ten thousand foot summit of the Transandine Railway linking Argentina and Chile.

A small brass plate on the coal bunker at the rear of the locomotive reveals that it was built the year before, 7000 miles away by Kitson & Co. in Leeds. The city was where the world's first commercially successful steam locomotives were constructed in 1812 by Fenton Murray & Wood at their Round Foundry in Holbeck for the nearby Middleton Colliery railway. Four locomotives were built and, like the Transandine engine, all worked on the rack system patented by John Blenkinsop.

In these early days of locomotive construction it was feared that a locomotive's adhesive weight alone would be insufficient to provide the necessary grip on the track, even on level ground.

The opening of the passenger-carrying Liverpool & Manchester Railway in 1830 marked the beginning of 'railway mania', attracting speculators and promoters keen to hitch a ride on what was to become a revolution within a revolution.

Yorkshire's first 'main line', the Leeds & Selby Railway, opened in 1834. Early railway companies were reliant on outside contractors to design and build their locomotives. The Leeds Round Foundry was well placed to provide the L&SR with its first locomotive '*Nelson*'. The company also constructed engines for the Liverpool & Manchester Railway, North Midland Railway and built a number of broad-gauge locomotives for Brunel's Great Western Railway.

One by one other locomotive builders took root in the Hunslet area of Leeds, starting with Todd, Kitson & Laird. One of their engines, '*Lion*',

The Kitson-Meyer articulated locomotives built by Kitson & Co. of Leeds, were truly remarkable machines. A set of cylinders and bogies at each end, made for a powerful and highly manoeuvrable locomotive, with examples working the tight curves and steep gradients of the South American Andes. The illustration shows one of the rack/adhesion variants built in 1909 to work on the Argentine Transandine Railway between Argentina and Chile.

built for the L&MR in 1838, became the star of the 1952 Ealing Studios' comedy '*The Titfield Thunderbolt*'.

The early history of railway engine building in Leeds was one of continual change. Former apprentices and employees of one company moved on to work for, or establish other workshops. Shepherd & Todd founded in 1839, had ceased to exist by 1846, but their Railway Foundry became home to E.B. Wilson, one of Leeds' early success stories.

At a time when companies were producing off-the-shelf designs, Wilson's chief draughtsman, David Joy, created one of Britain's first 'classic' express locomotive types. Named after a popular artiste of the day, the prototype, '*Jenny Lind*' was built in 1847 for the London Brighton & South Coast Railway. Ultimately over seventy of the class were built and sold to a number of Britain's principal railway companies.

Despite this apparent success, E.B. Wilson was wound up in 1858, paradoxically at a time when the major players in Yorkshire's locomotive building industry were in the ascendancy.

Kitson & Company, Manning Wardle, John Fowler & Co., Hudswell Clarke & Co. and the Hunslet Engine Company were based in Leeds. A huge shopping mall now stands in Sheffield where Yorkshire's 'other' locomotive builder, the Yorkshire Engine Company, established their Meadowhall Works in 1865.

Much of Britain's expanding railway network was being built by contractors using locomotives from the railway engineering workshops of Yorkshire. The railway companies themselves were starting to build their own engines. The order books of Leeds and Sheffield locomotive builders would begin to reflect Britain's growing reputation in railway engineering.

British industry was booming. Mines, steelworks, docklands, and slate quarries were looking for small, powerful steam locomotives to work their own internal railway networks. Yorkshire's engine builders supplied

OPPOSITE PAGE: 'Will Shakspeare' (sic), built by Leeds locomotive builders, E.B. Wilson and sold off-the-shelf to the Oxford, Worcester & Wolverhampton Railway in 1856. The locomotive is a member of the famous 'Jenny Lind' class designed by David Joy, one of Britain's little known and unsung railway engineers.

ABOVE: Early twentieth century steam power encounters a mode of transport from India's distant past. A world away from its birthplace, the Boyne Engine Works of Manning Wardle & Co. Ltd. Leeds, a 0-6-2 tank engine passes a row of traditional ox-carts beside the 27 miles long 2' 6" gauge Futwah-Islampur Light Railway. Photographed in 1982 the locomotive had far outlasted its builders who closed down in 1927. Sadly – unlike the ox-carts – neither locomotive nor railway line made it into the twenty first century.

RIGHT: Yorkshire's independent railway workshops made the transition from steam to diesel traction and continued to supply home and overseas markets. A metre gauge diesel locomotive built in 1939 by The Hunslet Engine Co. Ltd. Leeds, hauls a short freight train on the Guaqui-La Paz Railway, Bolivia.

hundreds of locomotives to a wide variety of industries. The majority were rugged four and six-wheeled tank engines. The Hunslet 'Austerity' 0-6-0 saddle tank designed for the Ministry of Supply is arguably the most successful locomotive designed in Leeds. Its no-frills wartime pedigree enabled hundreds of these machines to be built – many by other locomotive builders – between 1943 and 1964.

Within thirty years of the first four-and-a-half mile trial run of Blenkinsop's rack locomotive *Prince Regent*, two Leeds built engines were running on the Paris-Orleans railway. Supplying locomotives to a

The grimness of the surrounding industrial landscape only serves to highlight the superb workmanship and finish lavished on a Furness Railway express tank locomotive, as it emerges from the Airedale Foundry of Kitson & Co. Hunslet, Leeds, in the late 1920s.

developing industrial world became one of engineering's most competitive arenas. Leeds and Sheffield faced competition from both British and European builders.

Nineteenth century railway pioneers were opening up new routes, promoting economic growth through the transportation of goods and natural resources.

Some of the world's railway systems adopted the British standard gauge of 4ft 8½ in. There were also numerous narrow gauge lines, with track widths ranging from 1ft 11½in. to 3ft 6in.

In some countries narrow gauge meant anything but 'small', with narrow gauge engines working long distance main line services.

Hundreds of steam and diesel locomotives have been despatched from Yorkshire engine builders to standard and narrow gauge railways throughout the world including India, Africa, Spain, Egypt, South America, and Russia. Hunslet's first export in 1866 was a small saddle tank destined for a sugar plantation in Java. A similar engine built by the company in 1984 turned out to be the last commercially built steam locomotive in the western world – it too was bound for Java.

In the past, narrow gauge railways could be found in many parts of Britain and Ireland. Extensive narrow gauge systems worked the slate quarries of North Wales. The legacy of these former industrial lines can now be experienced and appreciated by visitors to the 'little railways' of North Wales. The Ffestiniog Railway, Talyllyn Railway, and the Welsh Highland Railway have survived to become world tourist attractions.

Manning Wardle, and Kitson & Co. disappeared from the Leeds engineering scene in the inter-war years. Hunslet, Hudswell Clarke, John Fowler and the Yorkshire Engine Company gradually moved into diesel locomotive production. For a time steam and diesel locomotives were being built simultaneously, until the fires were damped and finally dropped for steam.

Diesel locomotives had been built in Leeds since the 1930s. A small batch, built by Hunslet and Hudswell Clarke, were trialled by the LMS for shunting duties. After the Second World War, railways throughout the world began their unremitting progress towards diesel and electric traction. The skills and experience of Yorkshire's engine builders successfully adapted to new challenges, diversifying into new areas of engineering. However, world markets were changing, in ways that would influence the demise or survival of onetime cornerstones of industry.

Yorkshire Engine Company's closure in 1965 heralded further seismic changes. Shortly after, Hunslet, one of the world's most prolific and successful independent loco builders took Fowler and Hudswell Clarke under its wing, before further rounds of 'corporate restructuring' brought the long, complex, competitive history of locomotive building in Yorkshire to the buffer stops.

TOP: The coming of the railways turned Yorkshire's fishing towns and villages into holiday resorts and tourist destinations. Robin Hood's Bay, featured on this poster by Frank Sherwin, was on the line between Whitby and Scarborough.

BELOW: The Railway Preservation Movement and tourism have saved a number of Yorkshire branch lines. Grosmont Station is on the North Yorkshire Moors Railway. On the right is an industrial locomotive built in 1904 by Kitson & Co. of Leeds for the Lambton, Hetton & Joicey Collieries, County Durham.

ABOVE: Gresley A4 Streamlined Pacific 'Golden Shuttle', built by the LNER at their Doncaster Locomotive Works in 1937 to haul the 'West Riding Limited' between Bradford, Leeds and London. Later named 'Dwight D Eisenhower', the locomotive can now be seen at the US National Railroad Museum, Wisconsin.

BELOW: An A2 class locomotive is lowered onto its driving wheels in the erecting shop at Doncaster Locomotive Works in 1948.

EAST COAST THOROUGHBREDS

The railway map of Britain was still work in progress, when in 1848 Doncaster M.P. Edmund Denison persuaded the Great Northern Railway to include the town on its London to York route. Doncaster's rightful place in the firmament of Britain's railway history was assured when five years later, at Denison's behest, the GNR made the decision to re-locate its locomotive and carriage repair works from Boston in Lincolnshire to Doncaster in 1853.

The new railway works, or 'The Plant' as it became known, began by building new coaches but continued to concentrate on locomotive repair and maintenance. Outside contractors were engaged to build the company's new locomotives.

This was to change in 1866 with the appointment of a new locomotive superintendent – Patrick Stirling – subsequently described as 'a supreme artist among locomotive engineers', which coincided with the start of locomotive building in Doncaster designed and built to fulfil the demands of a wide variety of passenger and freight traffic.

Stirling and many of his contemporaries defined the first 'golden age'

With their 8ft driving wheels and graceful lines, Patrick Stirling's 'Singles' were every bit as speedy as they looked, playing an important role in the Great Northern Railway's participation in the famous 'Races to the North' in 1888 and 1895.

of steam locomotive design in Britain, creating some of the most beautiful machines ever to run on rails. Stirling's famous bogie 'Singles' firmly established the Doncaster locomotive racing pedigree later associated with *Flying Scotsman* and *Mallard*.

With their 8ft driving wheels, these raffishly elegant locomotives helped the Great Northern and its partners on the East Coast Route to match their West Coast rivals in the famous London to Edinburgh 'Races to the North' – the first of which occurred in 1888. Competitive running enabled both sides to achieve reduced journey times, with East Coast trains covering the 393 miles between London and Edinburgh in 6 hours 48 minutes, including a lunch stop at York, averaging 57.7mph.

The opening of the Forth Bridge in 1890 sparked off a further bout of racing; this time to Aberdeen in 1895. Again the contest caught the attention of the media and the public, who viewed it as a highly publicised sporting event. Gradually, the widespread introduction of smoother riding bogie coaches, meant that passenger comfort began to take precedence over speed.

In 1923 the independent railway companies in Britain merged to become the 'big four' – GWR, LMS, SR and LNER which included the Great Northern Railway. In the following year the LNER unveiled one of its latest locomotive at the Empire Exhibition, Wembley. Of the thousands who gazed in admiration, few would realise that this Doncaster built masterpiece of railway engineering would become the world's most famous steam locomotive – No.4472 *Flying Scotsman*.

No other steam locomotive before or since, has aroused the public consciousness. The word 'legend' has been conferred on both the locomotive and its designer Nigel Gresley. The phenomenon completely eclipsed the worthiness of the rest of the A1/A3 class, many of which were, in an inspirational example of publicity, named after winners of the Doncaster St Leger, the world's oldest 'classic' in the horse racing

calendar, first run in 1776 on Cantley Common.

Using a special corridor tender that enabled crews to be changed en-route, *Flying Scotsman* made the first ever non-stop run between London and Edinburgh in 1928. By 1934 the locomotive established the first authenticated 100mph record for steam traction in Britain. This new quest for speed and its obvious prestige value heralded a truly momentous era in Doncaster's locomotive building history.

Streamlining had begun to influence the exterior shape of aircraft, airships and cars. In Germany and the USA, high-speed diesel and electric railcars a few coaches in length – but built as a complete unit – were using aerodynamics to good effect. Gresley stayed loyal to steam, translating the concept into a powerful combination for the LNER's prestigious East Coast route.

The *Silver Jubilee* train commemorating the Jubilee of King George V and Queen Mary entered service on 1 October 1935. Armchair seating and a first-class restaurant cosseted passengers as they sped between London, Kings Cross and Newcastle.

The train was an immediate success and set the style for two other high-speed trains: the *Coronation*, running between London and Edinburgh, and the *West Riding Limited* linking Bradford and Leeds with the capital.

The external lines and colour schemes of the three trains followed through to match the locomotive hauling them. Once again, Nigel Gresley – who was knighted in 1935 – rose to the occasion. Streamlining and steam power were never better allied, than on his magnificent A4 Pacifics. A Bugatti racing car and wind tunnel testing influenced the striking aerodynamic wedge- shape of No. 2509 *Silver Link*, the first of the class to appear.

The locomotive immediately raised the bar for express passenger haulage in Britain by reaching 112mph twice, on the trial run of the Silver Jubilee in September 1935.

The A4's, all Doncaster built, and aptly nick-named 'streaks' by train spotters, were accorded maximum celebrity status by enthusiasts on station platforms or at engine sheds and line-side vantage points. An event on Sunday 3 July 1938 would ensure that one A4 in particular would achieve lasting immortality.

During brake testing on the East Coast Main Line, the crew of Gresley A4 No 4468 gave their Doncaster thoroughbred its head. *Mallard* responded in dramatic fashion by reaching 126mph and creating an unassailable world speed record for a steam locomotive.

The breadth of engineering skills inherent in Doncaster Locomotive

Works made it admirably suited to contributing to the war effort of both World Wars. In 1948 the LNER became part of British Railways, presaging the steady decline of steam power on Britain's railways. The floodgates had been gingerly opened at the plant in 1944, with the construction of four diesel-electric shunting locomotives. From the 1960s electric express passenger and diesel-electric heavy freight locomotives were being built at Doncaster.

Sadly the Plant built its last steam locomotive in 1957. Something more than mere sentiment has ensured that out of the thousands built there, a chosen few, including; *Mallard*, *Flying Scotsman*, and a Stirling 8ft 'Single', are still with us; tangible links between transport and social history, and a testament to the skills and craftsmanship inherent in supreme engineering.

TOP: A number of Doncaster's A3 Pacific's were fittingly named after winners of the town's famous St Leger classic. The fireman of No. 60050 Persimmon. replenishes the locomotives water supply during a stop at York in June 1960.

ABOVE: Owned by HM Edward VII, and ridden by Jack Watts, Persimmon won the St Leger in 1896.

IN THE LAP OF
THE GODS

Working in France in 1908, Leeds born engineering graduate Robert Blackburn (1885-1955) watched flying displays by Louis Bleriot, Wilbur Wright and Henry Farman. Combining a passion for aeroplanes and an engineer's enquiring mind, he quickly progressed from being an interested spectator to join these and other pioneer aviators by becoming a designer and builder of aircraft himself.

Photographed standing beside one of his monoplanes in 1913, Robert Blackburn had by then become well known in aviation circles. His commitment to flying led him to form the Blackburn Flying School at Filey on the Yorkshire coast.

The Blackburn Aircraft Company went on to specialise in military and naval aircraft, producing some of the most original and successful designs in British aviation history, from the days of the open cockpit to the streamlined jet-age.

Most of Yorkshire, and indeed the rest of the world, carried on regardless, when in 1853 at Brompton Dale near Scarborough, a petrified coachman flew a few hundred yards through the air in something resembling a boat on wheels suspended by a wooden framework beneath a fabric canopy.

Designated as a 'governable parachute' by its creator Sir George Cayley, it was in fact a man-carrying glider. The camber of the glider's wing meant that air flowed at a greater velocity over its upper surface than below, creating 'lift' – the principle behind the flying capability of every fixed-wing aeroplane.

Born in Scarborough in 1773, Cayley had been working on the aerodynamics of flight for some time. These early experiments are now recognised as the first steps in the development of heavier-than-air flight.

Over the next fifty years through the work of pioneers like Germany's Otto Lilienthal, gliding became the stepping stone to powered flight. After first experimenting with gliders in 1900, the Wright brothers made the world's first sustained and controlled powered flight at Kill Devil Hills, Kitty Hawk, North Carolina, in 1903.

Six years later in 1909, Frenchman Louis Bleriot coaxed his single engined monoplane across the English Channel. By October of that year the Doncaster Air Races attracted thousands hoping to witness the exciting but risk laden world of the aviators and their aeroplanes.

At this stage, the majority viewed the aeroplane as a source of sport and entertainment, rather than a machine with a potentially world-changing commercial or military future. Flying shows and air races began to attract large crowds who flocked to watch the likes of Samuel Franklin Cody, a professional showman of American origin who curiously became the first person to fly a powered aeroplane in Britain.

Cody, Wright, Bleriot, Cobham and A.V. Roe – names frequently seen on the programmes of early flying displays – were an inspiration to those who found themselves inexorably drawn to a challenge where manuals and textbooks were non-existent.

With no fewer than eight men holding it down, and its 80hp Gnome engine straining at the leash, a Blackburn Type 1 Monoplane prepares for take-off at the start of the 1913 War of the Roses Air Race. Sponsored by the Yorkshire Evening News, *the race covered a hundred mile circular course, connecting Leeds, Doncaster, Sheffield and Barnsley.*

During these early years of aviation history, before the public at large were tempted to put their trust in these 'new fangled flying machines', air races drew large crowds of spectators to witness what must have been one of the world's most dangerous sports. The technology was still largely untested, and airframe and engine reliability left much to be desired. These brave men and women, by their daring and skill were the catalyst in the early development of civil and military aviation.

The race steward 'striking a pose' on the left of the picture, is probably signalling to the race's other competitor, the pilot of an Avro 504 biplane; which, although advanced for its time was eventually beaten by the Blackburn Type 1, resulting in Robert Blackburn's first air-racing success.

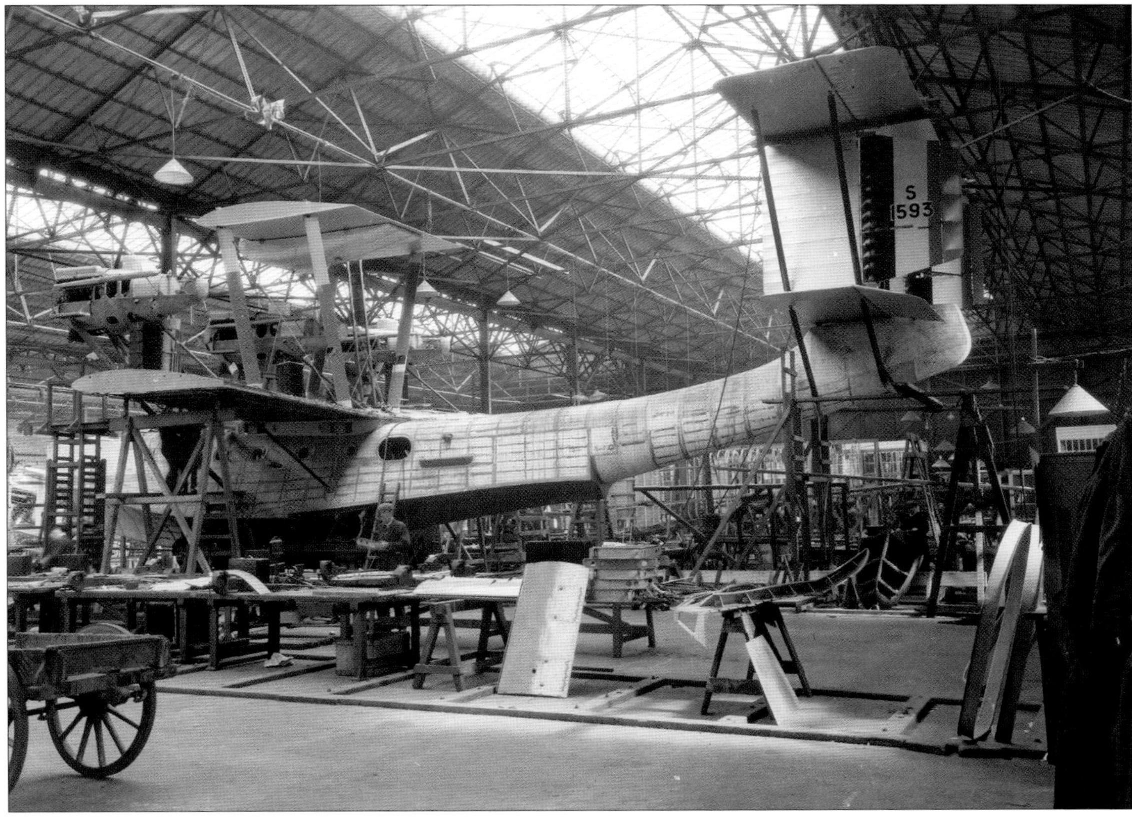

OPPOSITE PAGE: In 1909 Louis Bleriot crossed the English Channel in an open cockpit monoplane. Less than two decades later the crew of a Blackburn Iris long-range reconnaissance flying boat endure a similarly cold and windswept working environment as they patrol Britain's coastline. Known as 'Britain's Aerial Battleship', the prototype Iris first flew in 1926. Powered by three Rolls-Royce engines and costing £60,000 each, Iris flying boats were, at the time, the largest aircraft in service with the RAF.

RIGHT: Wooden trestles support the fuselage of an Iris III flying boat under construction at Blackburn's Brough works on Humberside in the 1920s.

The spirit of improvisation revealed itself on the sands between Saltburn and Marske in 1910 when Leeds born Robert Blackburn took to the controls of his 'First Monoplane' seated in a wicker garden chair. The engine fired into life and the machine taxied along the foreshore, picking up sufficient speed to briefly become airborne before slewing to one side and crashing.

Undaunted by this early set-back Blackburn pressed on, building further monoplanes. Test flights from Filey Sands and fields to the north of Leeds brought continual improvement and valuable experience, laying the foundations for what would eventually become Yorkshire's most successful aircraft builder.

Robert Blackburn became regularly involved in flying diplays and air races. Aircraft frequently crashed, but he and his fellow airmen continued to pin their faith in the commercial future of the steadily evolving aeroplane industry.

Business began to expand rapidly, resulting in the need for larger premises, eventually moving into the famous Olympia Works, a former skating rink in Roundhay Road, Leeds, in 1914.

The North Sea, always seen as a deterrent to would be invaders, failed to impede the torment meted out by German Zeppelins and U-boats in the First World War.

Yorkshire became a base for squadrons of Royal Flying Corps and Royal Naval Air Service aircraft flying reconnaissance and anti-submarine patrols. The county also became a centre for aircraft construction. Over a hundred BE2c biplanes were built at Blackburn's Olympia Works. Charles Portass & Sons, Sheffield, produced examples of the famous Sopwith Snipe and in Bradford, the Phoenix Dynamo Works of P.J. Pybus and furniture makers Christopher Pratt & Sons built aircraft, including a number of large Felixtowe flying boats.

The development of aircraft fitted with floats, enabling them to operate from water, has paralleled that of their wheeled land-based counterparts. Throughout the first half of the twentieth century, seaplanes and flying boats were seen as an alternative military and commercial option.

Blackburn's Olympia Works in Leeds and its new factory at Sherburn-

TOP: *Built and developed at Brough in East Yorkshire, and first flown in 1958, the Blackburn Buccaneer became Britain's finest low level strike aircraft, capable of carrying a formidable array of conventional and nuclear weapons. The photograph from 1960 shows two early prototypes under test.*

ABOVE: *A motor coach emerges from the cavernous fuselage of a Blackburn and General Universal Freighter. First flown from Brough and re-christened the Blackburn Beverley, the forty seven examples built were used primarily as military transport aircraft.*

in Elmet had turned out a number of Sopwith Baby seaplanes. In 1916 the company decided to specialise in designing and manufacturing aircraft for the navy.

By building a factory and seaplane test centre at Brough on the River Humber, Blackburn instigated one of Britain's most important aircraft building centres, from which came a long line of Blackburn aircraft, including the Iris long-range reconnaissance flying boat, the first of which took off from the Humber in June 1926. The Iris was followed by two more similar triple engined seaplanes; the Perth and the Sydney.

Manufacturers like Blackburn worked primarily to specifications issued by the Air Ministry. An aircraft could go through the lengthy process of design, prototype manufacture and testing, only for it to be rejected by the 'powers that be'.

Blackburn were not immune from disappointment, but there were notable successes. The Blackburn Ripon biplane became the Fleet Air Arm's standard carrier based torpedo bomber in the 1930s. The seaplane variant of the Ripon served with the Finnish Air Force. Britain's first dive bomber, the Blackburn Skua was the Fleet Air Arm's first monoplane to operate from the deck of an aircraft carrier. In a dramatic attack, Skuas sank the German cruiser *Konigsberg* in Bergen harbour in April 1940.

When the Second World War started Yorkshire once again became strategically important in the nation's bid for air supremacy. A diversity of skills in aircraft construction and maintenance were called upon. At Yeadon near Bradford a vast camouflaged aircraft factory was built to produce, among others, the Avro Lancaster bomber.

Peace returned in 1945. In Feltham, Middlesex, General Aircraft Limited began work on a huge four-engined transport plane. The company was bought out by Blackburn in 1948 to become Blackburn and General Aircraft Limited.

The Universal Freighter – later to be renamed the Blackburn Beverley – first flew from Brough in June 1950, and dwarfed anything built by Blackburn before or since. Built primarily as a military heavy-lift aircraft to transport or drop troops and equipment, the Beverley could operate from the shortest and most basic of airstrips.

The Blackburn Beverley's feats of strength were diametrically opposed to the revolution going on in aviation at the time. The dawn of the 'jet-age' presented aircraft manufacturers with a new set of challenges, not least the breaking of the sound barrier. It was also, chillingly, the crucible of nuclear weaponry.

In 1953, the Admiralty were looking for a low level strike aircraft capable of carrying a guided anti-shipping missile or a nuclear weapon.

Blackburn's years of experience in designing and building aircraft for the Royal Navy came to an impressive climax in the twin-turbojet powered Buccaneer – arguably the most advanced low level strike aircraft of its day, and capable of approaching its target flying at high speed a few hundred feet above the ground.

First flying in 1958, the Buccaneer went on to operational front-line service with squadrons operating from Lossiemouth and the aircraft carriers HMS *Ark Royal* and HMS *Victorious*.

The Buccaneer became Blackburn's magnificent swan-song. In 1959 the company became part of the Hawker Siddeley Group. Robert Blackburn, whose early flying exploits had thrilled onlookers on the sands at Filey died in 1955. He lived long enough to see his company and aviation take another leap of faith towards a rapidly changing and ever shrinking world.

ABOVE: A pair of Slingsby Tutor sailplanes dating from the 1940s.

The momentous flight of Sir George Cayley's man-carrying glider down Brompton Dale in 1853 was not only a significant milestone in aviation history, but the beginning of Yorkshire's noteworthy association with gliders and gliding. Controlled, powered flight eventually became a reality, but to some however, 'mastery of the air' meant working with the forces of nature to master flying in its purest form.

In 1931, ex RFC gunner and Scarborough furniture maker Frederick Slingsby took his first steps towards aviation greatness by building a German Falke glider.

The popularity of gliding clubs in the 1930s contributed to Slingsby abandoning furniture making to concentrate on glider production. By 1934 he had moved from premises in Scarborough's former tram shed, to a new factory at Kirby Moorside.

Slingsby Sailplanes Ltd. went on to build gliders based on their own designs, producing among others, the Kirby Kite, Cadet, Tutor, and the Gull, one of Britain's outstanding high-performance gliders. Countless Air Training Corps cadets were introduced to flying by the Slingsby sailplanes.

Sadly, the company produced its last glider in 1982, but Slingsby sailplanes still soar silently and gracefully over Britain.

LEFT: Sir George Cayley's man-carrying glider with his coachman at the helm, takes to the air in Brompton Dale, a few miles west of Scarborough.

LONG HAUL LEVIATHAN

At ten minutes to midnight on the 6th June 1915, in the sky a few thousand feet above Hull, a gigantic 500ft long torpedo shaped craft released a number of parachute flares, illuminating the complex network of docks below. Zeppelin L9 then fulfilled its sinister presence by dropping high explosive and incendiary bombs. In the ensuing conflagration, twenty five people lost their lives and forty five were wounded.

Rigid airships – or 'Zeppelins' as they became known – continued their raids on England and Scotland. Hull, Goole, York and Skinningrove were targeted in Yorkshire. Until the cessation of hostilities in 1918, airships were seen as monstrous purveyors of death and destruction. Their creator, Count Ferdinand von Zeppelin pioneered rigid-airship development. In recognising their military and commercial potential Zeppelin ensured Germany's pre-eminence in airship technology.

ABOVE: The immense size of the R100 airship and the shed in which it was constructed can be realised by the tiny figures of the two workmen in the foreground of this photograph taken at Howden in 1929.

Political indecision ensured that only a handful of rigid airships were built in Britain during the First World War, although our designers were benefitting from technical information acquired from captured or crashed German Zeppelins.

At last in 1919, those in Britain who put their faith in airships were rewarded when R34, built in Scotland by Beardmore, made the first ever double Atlantic crossing by air. Sadly, two years later, on a trial flight over Hull, R38 broke up and crashed in flames into the Humber. This awful spectacle, witnessed by many people in Hull, claimed the lives of 44 people.

For a time, airship flying in Britain ceased. However, its future as a luxury long distance mode of transport was being plotted. None was more enthusiastic than Charles Dennistoun Burney who persuaded Vickers to back him, forming a subsidiary company; the Airship Guarantee Company. Burney's persistence in political circles was rewarded by the Labour Government's decision to authorize the building of two airships. The R100 would be built by private enterprise and the R101 by the government, at Cardington, Bedfordshire.

In 1924 Vickers' Airship Guarantee Company was awarded the contract for the R100 and chose as a base a former First World War airship base at Howden, twenty miles west of Hull

Barnes Wallis – who was later to design the famous 'bouncing bomb' for the 'dambusters' raids of 1943 – was appointed chief designer. Wallis, who had worked for Vickers in the past, was considered to be Britain's foremost airship designer. Neville Shute Norway – better known as the novelist Neville Shute – joined the team as chief calculator.

Hundreds of people were involved in the construction of the R100, bringing prosperity to Howden and the surrounding area. Thousands paid a shilling each to gaze in awe as the airship took shape in the cathedral like space of its enormous shed.

A Boeing 747 'jumbo' jet would have been dwarfed by the 709ft length and 132ft diameter bulk of the R100. To achieve the required strength and lightness, the airship's framework was made of duralumin, a light aluminium alloy. The ship's gas bags, designed to hold five million cubic feet of hydrogen gas were made in Germany, and held in a specially designed spiral mesh net. This geodetic principal would later be applied by Barnes Wallis to the so called 'indestructible' Wellington bomber.

Six Rolls-Royce Condor petrol engines totalling 4,200hp could push the R100 along at 80mph – infuriatingly slow by today's jet-age expectations, but the airship's 3,500mile range far exceeded that of

Two giants of the sky: a unique moment in aviation history. April 1930, and crowds gather to witness Yorkshire's R100 airship at the mooring mast at Cardington, Bedfordshire, in the company of the world's most successful airship, Graf Zeppelin. Later that year, R100 would make a triumphal return flight to Montreal, Canada.

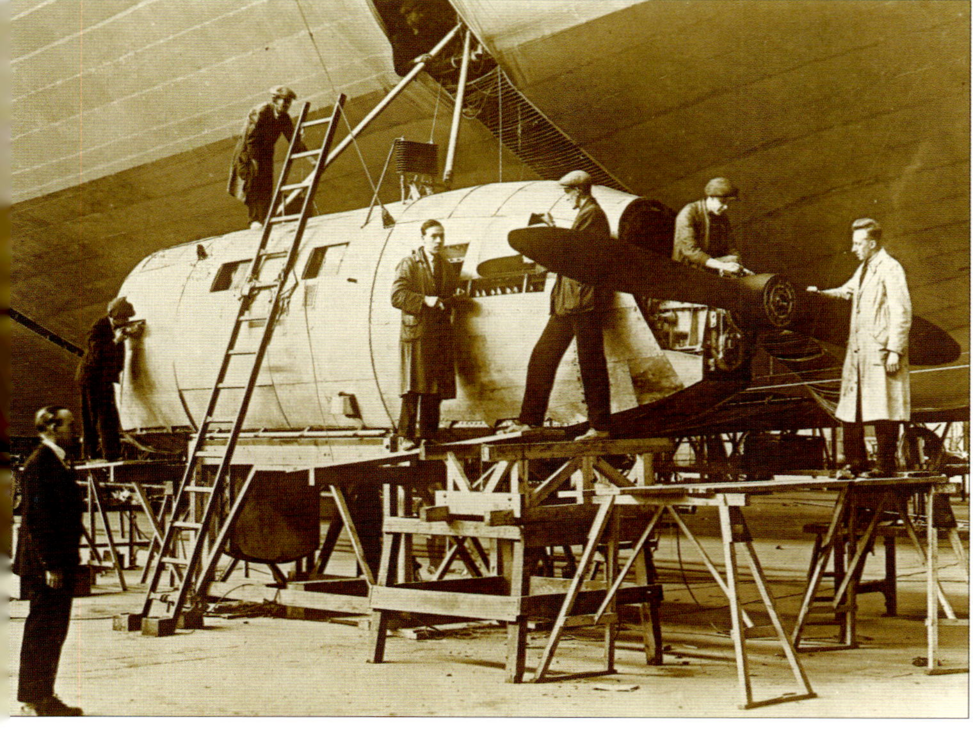

passenger aircraft at the time.

Airships could be boarded at ground level, but an alternative method involved ascending a mooring mast before stepping out onto a gangway to enter the airship through a door in its nose.

The R100 was designed to carry a hundred passengers in accommodation rivalling that of ocean liners, with electrically lit and heated two and four-berth cabins, dining room, kitchen and promenade deck. At the time, the R100 and R101 were seen as the future of transcontinental air travel. Scheduled flights to India, South Africa, Canada and Australia were envisaged.

It must have been an emotional and stirring sight for all concerned, when on the 16 December 1929 the R100 emerged from its shed with the assistance of five hundred soldiers from the Yorkshire and Lancashire Regiment. The following day the airship took to the skies. A craft the size of the liner *Mauretania*, circling over York at a thousand feet, must have made an unforgettable sight.

The R100 flew to Cardington in preparation for its now celebrated return flight to Canada. Its arrival in Montreal on 1 August 1930 was greeted by a crowd of 30,000. Thousands of miles away from her native Yorkshire, the R100 had made a great impression, but sadly, the uneventful return journey to Cardington was destined to be the airships last.

The use of potentially flammable hydrogen gas in airships presented one of the greatest challenges to airship designers. America was the only source of the less volatile helium gas.

On the 4 October 1930 sister ship R101 set out on her flight to India. A storm over Beauvais sent the airship into an uncontrollable dive before it hit the ground and burst into flames. Of the 54 on board only six survived.

After the triumph of the R100, the ascendant hopes and dreams of Britain's airship industry were also shattered on that French hillside. The British airship programme was abandoned and the R100 – Yorkshire's magnificent long haul leviathan – was dismantled and reduced to £450 worth of scrap metal.

OPPOSITE PAGE, TOP: Working on one of the airship's six 650hp Rolls-Royce Condor petrol engines.

OPPOSITE PAGE, BELOW: A close-up of the dining room of the R100 exemplifies the luxury of long distance airship travel.

ABOVE: The romance of transcontinental airship travel, personified by John Holroyd's moody photograph of the Taj Mahal. Routes linking Britain with India, Canada, South Africa and Australia were planned.

RIGHT: A tobacco jar made from the light alloy duralumin, by an apprentice working on the R100 at Howden.

FAR RIGHT: A commemorative booklet published in 1928 to coincide with a visit by members of parliament to Howden.

BRUTE FORCE AND FINESSE

The ability to create a cutting edge has been crucial to the survival of humankind. Metal knives and spears were fashioned to hunt for food and defend territory; sickles, scythes, shears and ploughs contributed to the development of stable communities.

Metal smelting began centuries before the so called 'industrial revolution'. The Cistercian monks of Kirkstall Abbey on the River Aire near Leeds began forging iron soon after the abbey was completed in 1182, starting a tradition that, after the Dissolution, was taken into private ownership and survived until 2002. Kirkstall Forge's 800 years of continual production is regarded as the longest in British history. But for unparalleled breadth and depth in the field of metallurgy, South Yorkshire, and one city in particular, stands supreme above the rest.

Sheffield's reputation as the nation's 'steel city' began with the pursuit of that important cutting edge. A pilgrim in Geoffrey Chaucer's fourteenth century *Canterbury Tales* is described as carrying a Sheffield thwitel (knife). More substantial records begin to appear from the sixteenth century, with 'the presence of many cutlers in Hallamshire' (the ancient district around Sheffield). The term 'cutler' defined as 'all persons using to make knives, blades, scissors, shears, sickles and cutlery wares made of wrought iron or steel.'

The rivers Don, Sheaf, Loxley, Porter and Rivelin ensured a plentiful supply of water to power forges, tilt hammers and rolling mills. By the seventeenth century the area had the greatest concentration of cutlery trades in the land. In 1624 an Act of Incorporation created the Company of Cutlers – a governing body charged with overseeing apprenticeships, quality control, and ensuring the validity of craftsman's identifying marks. Specialisation was encouraged within the cutlery industry by the Company, whose remit extended to include the making of edge tools like files, saws and chisels. This growing group of craftsmen became known as 'Little Mesters'.

Blades, hand forged and made wholly of iron, began to be superseded by iron, edged by a thin strip of steel; a metal that retained a cutting edge better. The first generation of steel making in South Yorkshire began with

This slumbering giant of the steel industry's remarkable past now reposes in sylvan surroundings at Kelham Island Museum, Sheffield. The Bessemer Convertor patented in 1856 is one of the most significant inventions in the history of engineering. Turning iron into steel became cheaper and more plentiful through the Bessemer process. This, the last working Bessemer Convertor, ended its working life at British Steel Corporation's Workington Works, Cumbria, in 1974. The car parked beneath the convertor's towering bulk represents late twentieth century technology, where steel and glass can now be blended into subtle curves.

the production of cementation steel. Bars of wrought iron were packed in charcoal and fired in a brick, bottle-shaped furnace; the carbon from the charcoal being absorbed by the bars of iron. The incorporation of steel into the manufacture of cutlery and edge tools resulted in improved products; but cementation steel, prone to blistering, was less than perfect. The efforts of a Quaker clockmaker were to elevate steelmaking to a higher plane.

Frustration at working on clock mechanisms with inferior German or Swedish steel led Benjamin Huntsman to search for a better solution. 1742, the year in which Huntsman moved from Doncaster to Sheffield, will be forever one of the most crucial in the city's history. Huntsman's experiments, conducted over several years, involved re-melting cementation steel in clay pots or crucibles. After skimming off impurities, the molten steel could then be poured into ingot moulds – the first time this had been achieved with steel. Though crucible steel could only be made in relatively small quantities, this significant advance in quality laid the foundation for South Yorkshire's eventual rise to pre-eminence in world steelmaking.

As Benjamin Huntsman toiled to perfect crucible steel, Thomas Boulsover, a Sheffield cutler, was pursuing a metallurgical goal of a different kind. In 1743 he discovered that by fusing a thin sheet of silver onto a thicker sheet of copper the result looked like solid silver, and could be produced at considerably less cost. Old Sheffield Plate, as it became known, grew into a major industry, producing ornamental buckles, snuff boxes, candlesticks, coffee pots and other decorative tableware. A number of companies manufacturing plated ware diversified into making items of solid silver. Well over four hundred people were working in both trades by the 1770s, justifying the opening of the Sheffield Assay Office in 1773.

A century after it was first discovered Old Sheffield Plate was superseded by electroplating – a technique using an electric current to deposit silver on a base metal.

The contrasting discoveries and development of crucible steel and Old Sheffield Plate took place against a background of expansion in the iron industry, where coke was replacing charcoal in the smelting process. The huge reserves of the South Yorkshire Coalfield were set to ignite the fires of industrial expansion. Steam power, whose engines were first created by the iron industry, would change the world of work forever, liberating industry from riverside locations and eventually precipitating the demise of canal building; directing teams of 'navvies' towards the construction of a growing railway network.

Textile mills, bridges, aqueducts, railways and shipbuilding increased in size and scale thanks to iron and the power of steam. In 1854 cast iron plating for Brunel's SS *Great Eastern* was produced by Samuel Beal and Co., Park Gate Ironworks, Rotherham. Iron's supreme role as the material of the Industrial Revolution would ultimately be challenged in the heat of a 'super crucible' called the Bessemer converter.

Hertfordshire born, Henry Bessemer announced his revolutionary invention for creating cheap steel in 1856. Bessemer's converter – an enormous open-ended vessel lined with ganister clay – turned molten pig-iron into steel by blasting air through it. This burnt off the carbon and other elements. It was now possible to make steel in greater volume at about a fifth of the cost of crucible steel.

Bessemer was keen to persuade other steelmakers to take out licences and install their own converters. Choosing Sheffield in which to open his Bessemer Steel Works in 1858 established South Yorkshire as a world centre for the production of steel on an unprecedented scale.

Although there was still a valuable market for good quality crucible steel, the high volume potential of Bessemer steel presented an attractive proposition to manufacturers in South Yorkshire and further afield, on Teesside.

John Brown & Co. was the first in Sheffield to install Bessemer convertors. Railways were spreading around the globe, providing South Yorkshire iron and steel firms with a lucrative market. Brown's made their first batch of Bessemer steel rails in 1860.

A decade after the first Bessemer convertors discharged their melts of cheap steel a rival process came on the scene. William Siemens pioneered his open-hearth furnace in South Wales. In this process iron ore was added to molten cast iron and scrap steel. Modifications could be made as the melt progressed, ensuring that the finished product was of higher quality than Bessemer steel. Steelmakers throughout the land were quick to add Siemens furnaces to their production lines.

Unsurprisingly, Sheffield's total immersion in metallurgy would often provide the industry with inventions of significant consequence. By day Robert Hadfield worked in his father's Hecla Works steel foundry, using his spare time to perform experiments using a small furnace at home. In 1882 Hadfield discovered that steel with a 12.5% manganese content hardened with use. Manganese steel eventually outperformed others in the race to find ever more effective ordnance and armour plate.

From the 1860s the iron and steel industry became increasingly involved in the arms trade, largely due to the introduction of the first

ABOVE: Grinding scythe blades by hand using water powered machinery in the Rivelin Valley, Sheffield in the 1920s.

OPPOSITE PAGE, TOP: Cementation or 'blister steel' furnaces at Daniel Doncaster and Sons' Doncaster Street Works, Sheffield, in 1951, showing the dampers fitted during the Second World War to screen light from enemy aircraft.

OPPOSITE PAGE, BELOW: Crucible steel making in the East Forge melting shop at Cammell's Cyclops Works, Sheffield, in the 1890s. In the foreground, two workmen are pulling out and teeming molten steel from a crucible. Invented by Benjamin Humtsman in 1742, crucible steel laid the foundations for Sheffield's pre-eminence in the development and production of high quality steels.

Hadfield's and Thomas Firth, and Park Gate, Steel, Peech and Tozer in Rotherham were, between them, producing weapons of war on a diverse and gigantic scale; ranging from machine guns and anti-aircraft guns to 15-inch naval guns capable of hurling a 1,900lb projectile over thirty miles. Millions of shells were produced by women employed throughout the steel industry in wartime.

The post-war years saw manufacturing in decline. In Sheffield the steel industry re-grouped. Vickers-Armstrong and Cammell-Laird merged to become English Steel, whilst Thomas Firth and John Brown joined forces to become Firth Brown. By the mid-1930s political tensions in Europe brought re-armament to the Don Valley once more. Steelmaking, forging, and machining components for every aspect of our armed forces wartime operations were undertaken.

The development of special steels continued during the inter-war years; enabling, for instance, the Rolls-Royce Merlin aero engine to reach

ironclad warships armed with iron plated hulls over four inches thick. Ordnance manufacturers were provoked into producing projectiles of ever greater destructive power. The importance of the navy to iron and steel makers led to Cammell's acquisition of Laird Brothers shipyard, Birkenhead. John Brown began shipbuilding on the River Clyde and Vickers took over the naval construction yard in Barrow.

'The war to end all wars' began in 1914. Heavy industry cranked itself up to meet the challenge head-on. In vast works covering a considerable acreage, Sheffield's 'big five' – Vickers, John Brown, Cammell-Laird,

its legendary status in aviation.

Throughout both world wars the huge scale of military hardware production ran parallel to other demands – including machine tools – emphasising the importance of the extensive supporting role played by manufacturing in times of war.

Technical advances made in steelmaking during wartime benefited from large scale post-war modernisation. Gas-fired furnaces and electrically powered sheet mills and arc furnaces were part of the dawn of a new era that would create the nationalised British Steel Corporation – itself later privatised and today jointly owned by the Dutch company Corus and Indian steel producer, Tata. The 'leaner and fitter' mantra of business practice has indelibly changed the landscape of the steel industry.

The cutlery and edge tool industries, with their proliferation of small family run firms – many of whom resisted 'modernisation' were, in the end, unable to compete with cheaper imports from abroad. South Yorkshire's founding metallurgical industry was by the 1960s in decline; a

ABOVE: Forging presses, hammers, and rolling mills of immense size, produced armour plate, naval guns and armour-piercing shells for both World Wars in the iron and steel works of south Yorkshire's Don Valley. Firing her 16-inch guns, HMS Nelson *demonstrates the awesome power of naval gunnery and ballistics. Weighing 33,950 tons* HMS Nelson *was built by Armstrong Whitworth, Newcastle. Her sister ship* HMS Rodney *was built by Cammell Laird, Birkenhead. Both vessels were launched in 1927. (IWM A9284).*

OPPOSITE PAGE, LEFT: Dirt, grime, and the overpowering scale of the rolling machine she is operating, fail to diminish the smile of one of Mappin and Webb's employees working in spoon production in the 1920s.

OPPOSITE PAGE, RIGHT: George Clark of North British Works, Sheffield, produced this stylish cutlery in the 1930s. Designed by Douglas Clark, they were intended to be produced from one piece of flat sheet steel. Though striking in appearance they were less than successful, being not well balanced. A worthy exercise never the less, from a firm better known for producing steel for shovels, spades and saws.

corrosive process that would in due course spell the end of luminaries like Mappin and Webb, Walker & Hall and James Dixon & Sons.

Today, shoppers practice the art of retail therapy in the sprawling Meadowhall Shopping Centre, built on the site of Hadfield's East Hecla Works. In Rotherham, a retail park has replaced Parkgate Iron & Steel Works, and the former melting shop of Steel, Peech and Tozer has now become the Magna Science Adventure Centre. On a positive note, engineering components of unimaginable size and complexity continue to be produced at companies like Sheffield Forgemasters and Davey Markham.

Creativity on a more intricate scale involving the long practiced art of working with precious metals still continues and is looking to a distinguished future through the innovative work of students at Sheffield Hallam University.

The billowing smoke of industry has largely dispersed, but brute force and finesse still reside in Yorkshire's valley of steel.

On Yorkshire's northern border with County Durham, Joseph Pease and a group of likeminded Quaker industrialists extended the 1825 Stockton and Darlington Railway to the south bank of the River Tees. Here a number of staithes were built for the purposes of exporting coal from the Durham coalfield.

This example of pre-Victorian commercial enterprise became in 1830, the origins of the town of Middlesbrough. Coal exports, shipping, and a pottery, formed the nucleus of the town's industrial base until an ironworks set up by Henry Bolckow and John Vaughan in 1841 triggered the spectacular industrial expansion that made Middlesbrough the fastest growing town in nineteenth century Yorkshire.

Initially, Bolckow and Vaughan used imported ore, but the discovery of substantial deposits of ironstone in the nearby Cleveland hills in 1848 provided the impetus to boost production on Teesside. This same field of ironstone eventually brought blast furnaces to Skinningrove, adjacent to the iron mines at Loftus near Saltburn.

Other ironmasters joined Bolckow and Vaughan. Gilkes, Wilson and Pease, the Bell Brothers and Cochranes, became household names along the banks of the River Tees, where, by the 1870s there were over a hundred blast furnaces producing two million tons of pig iron. Before the end of the century however the booming iron industry in the north-east began to feel the impact of industrial change and the growing demand for steel. There was still a market for pig-iron, but it was a matter of survival that iron makers took on this new challenge.

Working with the huge forces harnessed by the iron and steel industries requires a high level of teamwork. Hammer man Albert French; second man Harry Grinold and driver Frank Hurst take a quick breather before resuming work with a steam hammer at Daniel Doncaster & Sons Ltd. Penistone Road, Sheffield, in the 1920s. Invented in 1839 by James Nasmyth, the steam hammer was a development of the water powered tilt hammer.

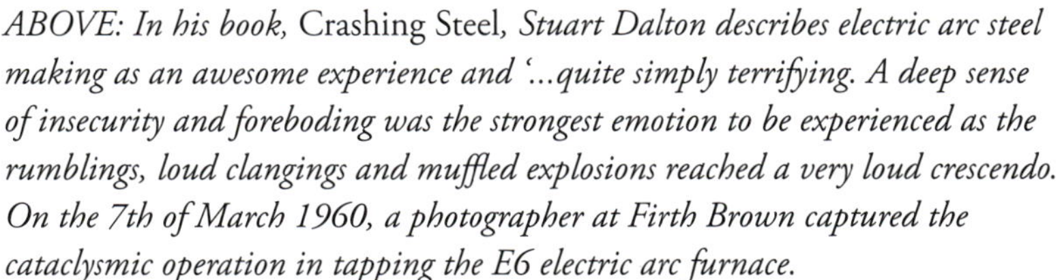

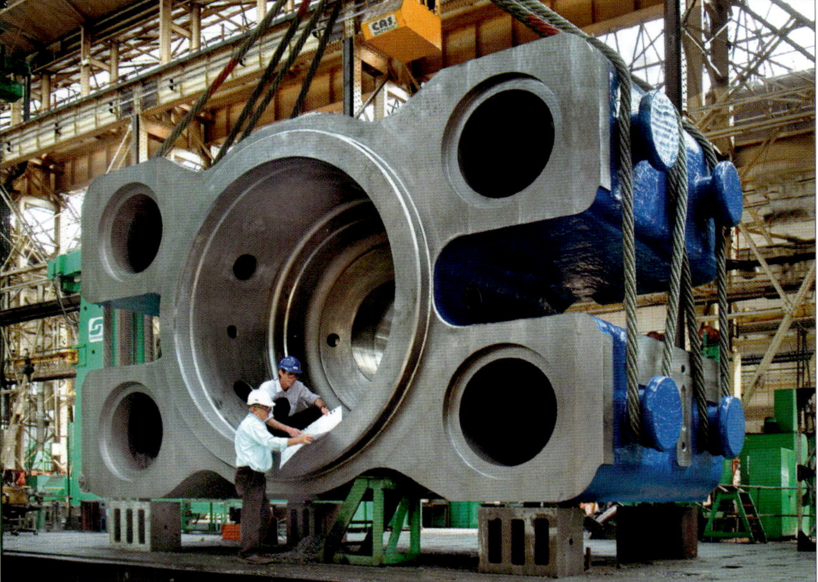

ABOVE: In his book, Crashing Steel, *Stuart Dalton describes electric arc steel making as an awesome experience and '...quite simply terrifying. A deep sense of insecurity and foreboding was the strongest emotion to be experienced as the rumblings, loud clangings and muffled explosions reached a very loud crescendo.' On the 7th of March 1960, a photographer at Firth Brown captured the cataclysmic operation in tapping the E6 electric arc furnace.*

TOP RIGHT: A computer controlled gantry milling machine was used in machining this 325 ton component intended for a huge German built screw press - an operation carried out in one of western Europe's largest engineering workshops at Davy Markham Limited, Sheffield.

RIGHT: Two well known Rotherham landmarks now gone. Photographed in 1965, the blast furnaces at Park Gate Iron & Steel Works towered over the surrounding area. 6,000 men were once employed by Park Gate, which underwent a steady decline in the 1970s prior to closure a decade later.

From an era when production was more important than pollution: an aerial photograph of Pease & Partners Normanby Ironworks taken in 1929 shows in fascinating detail a small area of the extensive iron and steel making activity spread along the south bank of the River Tees around Middlesbrough.

Almost two and a half centuries after cementation steel was first made in South Yorkshire, the ironmen in the north of the county began to grasp the new future that lay ahead in the manufacture of steel. Bolckow and Vaughan began producing steel by the Bessemer process. In 1875 this well-established company was joined in competition by a new firm headed by former ironworkers Arthur Dorman and Albert de Lande Long.

Dorman Long moved quickly into steel production with production reaching 100,000 tons a year by 1890. Expansion followed leading to the absorption of neighbouring companies, including Teesside stalwart, Bell Brothers in 1899. Eventually progress was such that, in 1929, the company merged with Bolckow and Vaugham; rescuing its old adversary from cripping debts. Now employing over 30,000 men, Dorman Long was ready to compete worldwide.

Few things celebrate the achievements of civil engineering more spectacularly than bridge building. Newcastle's Tyne Bridge opened in 1928. This graceful stone and steel structure, rivalling Stephenson's earlier High Level Bridge nearby, became Dorman Long's prelude to something even more impressive; the Sydney Harbour Bridge, Australia. Opened in 1932, this product of Yorkshire's River Tees has become a global emblem of the city of Sydney and one of the southern hemisphere's most memorable man-made landmarks. Dorman Long epitomise world-wide, the enduring legacy of iron and steelmaking on the south bank of the River Tees.

Working on developing steel for use in gun barrels in the research laboratories of steelmakers Brown-Firth in 1913, Harry Brearley found that low carbon steel containing around 12% chromium showed a resistance to corrosion. Brearley gave the name 'rustless steel' to his discovery. Sadly, a dispute over the rights of his invention led to Brearley's resignation from Firth's.

Rustless – or stainless steel – as the product became more widely known, was used almost immediately by the cutlery industry. A decade after it was first invented, Firth's began to market a further developed version under the name of 'Staybright' steel; becoming a highlight of the 1934 *Daily Mail* Ideal Homes Exhibition. The same year saw the launch of the Cunard liner, *Queen Mary* in which 'Staybright' steel was used to great effect in the ships interior decor.

It is impossible today to imagine the medical and surgical professions, or the food and drinks industries, operating without the benefits of stainless steel.

Described at the time as having a 'soft gleam', and with a distinctive tactile quality, stainless steel was – along with chrome, nickel plate and silver – destined to contribute to one of the twentieth century's most enduring cultural movements – Art Deco. Emanating from the 1925 Paris Exposition, Art Deco became a major stylistic influence in furniture, textile, jewellery, architecture, graphic and interior design throughout the world.

Harry Brearley's experience in metallurgy told him that his discovery could have wide ranging commercial possibilities, but even he could not have appreciated the continuing multifaceted contribution made by stainless steel to the modern world.

Looking like something from a science fiction film, the brooding bulk of Redcar No.1 blast furnace towers above a windswept frozen landscape. A powerful, almost surreal scene that fully justified Middlesbrough born photographer Ian Macdonald's midnight assignation with this monumental industrial giant capable of producing 10,000 tons of iron a day.

A cutlery classic: An original Firth Brearley stainless knife from the 1920s.
This example, like quite a few others is still in daily use.

OPPOSITE PAGE: The Chrysler Building in New York is regarded as an icon in world architecture,
a distinction achieved in no small measure by the use of stainless steel (discovered in Sheffield by
Harry Brearley in 1913) incorporated into the building's impressive Art Deco spire.

BELOW: In Britain, stainless steel made its own impact; from the nation's cutlery drawers to the
world of high society. When modernisation took place at London's Savoy Hotel in 1929 'Staybrite'
stainless steel was chosen for the entrance canopy.

DEEP HARMONY

Staithes in the twenty-first century is now a far cry from its position in the early nineteenth century when, as Yorkshire's largest fishing port, it was home to seventy coble boats and a number of larger sailing yawls and Yorkshire luggers.

Staithes and nearby Runswick have been an inspiration to scores of artists and photographers. The Staithes Group of Impressionist painters worked in the area between the 1870s and the early part of the twentieth century.

Every year, thousands make the journey to Yorkshire's east coast in search of sunshine and the bracing 'tang' of the sea. Beaches, cliff tops and promenades keep most of us firmly anchored on terra firma, providing safe vantage points from which to 'savour the view'. On less favourable days, we're apt to gaze with mingled awe and reverence on the mighty North Sea, whipped into a foaming frenzy and driven like a battering ram into cliffs and sea walls by a rampaging 'north-easterly'.

Here was the hunting ground of the county's once vast fishing fleet, working out of ports and harbours strung along the coast from the Humber to the Tees.

In the eighteenth century, fishing became of secondary importance in Whitby when the town became one of the country's leading shipbuilding ports, supplying vessels for the whaling, coal, iron and alum industries. Merchants and shipyard owners were supported by a multitude of trades including carpenters, sailmakers, ropers, blacksmiths and painters. All this commercial activity attracted the services of banks and insurance agents, bringing a measure of wealth to Whitby, whose economy in the nineteenth century was also bolstered by the jet industry.

The smaller fishing villages of Staithes, Runswick, Robin Hood's Bay, Flamborough and Filey, were almost totally dependent on fishing. When times were hard, fishermen looked for work in the local iron mines. Early in the nineteenth century, Staithes was the premier fishing port on the Yorkshire coast.

In the days of fishing under sail, the Yorkshire lugger and the yawl were the largest fishing vessels operating out of Staithes and other Yorkshire fishing ports. Both vessels had a reputation for speed; a virtue much appreciated by those intent upon outfoxing Customs and Excise officialdom.

When fishing for cod, haddock or herring, luggers and yawls carried two smaller coble boats on deck. Once the fishing grounds were reached these were lowered into the water to check the fishing nets or lines.

Luggers and yawls have, sadly, disappeared from Yorkshire's harbours, as has their successor, the steam trawler. Through times of great change in the fishing industry, the east coast coble has survived – albeit like the fish themselves – in much fewer numbers.

Craftsmanship and artistry combine with a singularity of purpose to encapsulate the classic lines of the English square sterned cable. EMBRACE WY207 was built in the 1960s for Staithes fisherman George Harrison and his son Neil by the late Gordon Clarkson, one of Whitby's long line of craftsman boat builders.

ABOVE: Boats from as far afield as Scotland and Cornwall found their way to Whitby during the herring season. In this nineteenth century photograph by Frank Meadow Sutcliffe, cobles share this peaceful view across the town's upper harbour with a group of visiting Scottish sailing luggers.

OPPOSITE PAGE, TOP: The end of an era: Fishing boat historian, Gloria Wilson's camera records Tony Goodall at work on his final coble at his Sandsend boatyard in 1992. INCENTIVE WY373 – Goodall's 180th boat – was built for Skipper Adrian Turnbull of Redcar.

OPPOSITE PAGE, BELOW: Until well into the twentieth century, fishermen – often with the help of their wives – used their own muscle power to launch and retrieve their vessels from the foreshore. Today, the ubiquitous combination of tractor and trailer is more likely to be employed. SHEENA WY796 takes to the sea of Sandsend.

The coble's clinker-built construction using overlapping planks suggests a possible Viking pedigree, and there is documented evidence relating to them being used in Elizabethan times.

The English square-sterned coble – to give it its correct title – is primarily an inshore fishing boat, propelled originally by oars and a single sail. Its ability to be launched and retrieved stern first directly from the foreshore has influenced the overall shape and design of the craft. Cobles can vary in length from ten to forty feet. The larger variants are known as 'ploshers'.

The front of the boat is finely shaped below the waterline to cut through the waves, whilst the outward curve of the hull above, gives the boat lift in heavy seas. Two sledge-like runners underneath enable it to be hauled over the beach.

To the untrained eye cobles may all look the same, but the builders themselves made their mark on the basic design by introducing their own subtle variations, and responding to fishermen's individual needs and preferences.

To those closest to them, these shapely vessels are apt to elicit words like: 'buxom', 'fullness' and 'eyesweet', in describing one of the finest examples of function and form in perfect unison.

The long era of sail gradually came to an end with the introduction of petrol and diesel motors. Wheelhouses and echo sounders have, in most cases, not impinged greatly on the timeless lines of these sturdy but functionally graceful craft.

While the men were at sea, it was the women and girls who, apart from cooking and cleaning, were responsible for gathering bait. This meant walking miles along their own and neighbouring foreshores collecting limpets and mussels which then had to be patiently removed from their shells and hooked on to fishing lines, each carrying well over five hundred hooks.

Non-Conformity became the bedrock of daily life in fishing villages like Staithes, Robin Hood's Bay and Filey. Revivalist meetings, love feasts and evangelical rallies, led by the stirring oratory of lay preachers, attracted crowds from miles around to both chapels, cliff tops and open fields.

Through the fishermen themselves, this intensity of feeling found its way to the shoreline. 'Galilee', 'Deep Harmony', 'Crimond' and Rock of Ages' – the Bible and hymn book proving to be an endless source of inspiration when conferring names on their coble boats.

Robin Hood's Bay Congregational Church, 1840. Non-Conformity played an important part in the spiritual and social life of Yorkshire's fishing villages.

ABOVE: Fishermen and onlookers gather at Coffee House Corner fish market, Whitby, in preparation for a fish auction.

BELOW: Women gathering 'flithers' or limpets as bait for long-line fishing. Sea coal and driftwood for fuel were also collected in this way.

The ever present dangers inherent in some industries have fostered a deep rooted unity among their working communities. Before science and technology began to play a vital part in safeguarding working lives, this communal bond was even stronger – and nowhere more so than among the inhabitants of our coastal fishing towns.

Setting out to sea to earn a living in a vessel of any kind, let alone a small wooden craft, relies on something more than experience and intuition. On the open sea, driving wind and rain are potent reminders of forces and influences far greater than ourselves. No wonder that a firm belief in a 'guiding hand' was so important to our fishermen and their families.

Nineteenth century preacher Robert Verrill of Staithes was an ancestor of Matt Verrill who first went to sea full-time in the STAR OF HOPE WY174 in 1928. Built by J.T. Cole, the coble was one of the last to be built in Staithes. The terrible storm of 1953 claimed the vessel, smashing her to pieces and issuing a reminder of a way of life constantly at the mercy of the awesome power of nature.

JOSEPH FOLJAMBE'S FORGOTTEN MASTERPIECE

Ploughing has always been at the heart of land management and food production. A furrow in the soil starts a chain reaction orchestrated by nature herself. Surface vegetation ploughed back into the land adds nutrients, leaving frost, wind and rain to break the soil down in readiness for seeding.

Based on a strong, almost square wooden frame, ploughs in medieval Britain were heavy and cumbersome often requiring up to ten oxen to drag them over the land. This somewhat over-engineered approach persisted until the eighteenth century.

History, in the main, has paid scant attention to Joseph Foljambe of Sheffield, who, by using a triangular frame, changed the basic geometry of the plough, making it dynamically more efficient. Light, but still strong, and requiring the power of only two horses, Foljambe's plough was both easier to handle and much faster than ploughs in general use at the time.

This future of this groundbreaking farm implement was assured when Foljambe formed a partnership with Disney Stanyforth, whose Rotherham property portfolio was founded on the inherited wealth from his father's iron trading business. In his role as entrepreneur, Stanyforth, at his own expense, applied for the plough's patent in 1730 and took on the responsibility of advertising it.

A factory was established in Rotherham – from which the plough took its name – to produce three hundred ploughs a year using parts based on master patterns. This production line method of manufacture made the Rotherham plough one of the first agricultural implements to be put into mass production.

The Rotherham plough set a new benchmark in plough design and construction, and is a prime example of how a fresh eye on a subject can lead to further refinement and improvements.

James Arbuthnot, a Norfolk farmer, came close to producing the ultimate 'Rotherham' by using mathematical calculations to determine the optimum shape of the mouldboard – the part of a plough carrying

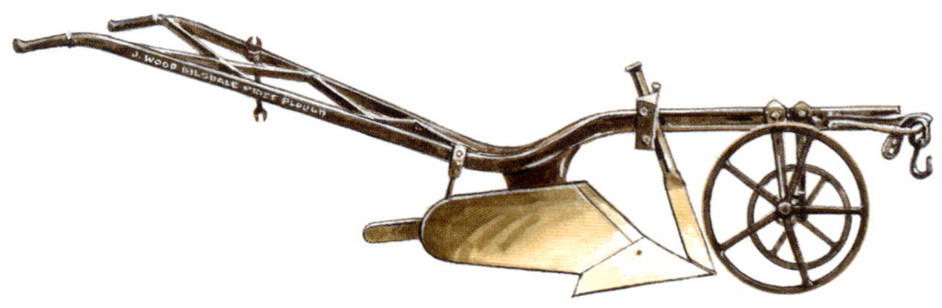

TOP : Popular in east and north Yorkshire, the North Cave plough was a variant of the Rotherham plough. This particular example photographed by Frank Meadow Sutcliffe would have been made by local craftsmen.

ABOVE: A lightweight iron-framed plough by the well known north Yorkshire plough maker John Wood of Bilsdale (north of Helmsley), who moved his business to Driffield in 1911. A contemporary catalogue prices the plough at £7.12s 6d.

the share or blade.

Others, like Scotsman, James Small, brought their own improvements to the original design; confirming that, despite the influences of 'new thinking' most ploughs were made by local craftsmen with the nature of the local land in mind.

After 1800, iron-framed ploughs began to replace their predominantly timber built antecedents. Regional preferences continued to be incorporated, but in overall line and form, all acknowledged that Joseph Foljame's original had enabled agriculture to plough a new and more profitable furrow.

ABOVE : The final development of the Rotherham plough by James Arbuthnot, a Norfolk farmer who used mathematical calculations to further improve the performance of Joseph Foljambe's revolutionary Rotherham plough.

A NEW POWER ON THE LAND

In an area of south-east Leeds, where mining and farming existed side-by-side, a Fowler seven-furrow anti-balance disc plough is shown on trial in 1923. A range of cultivating equipment including: ploughs, harrows, scarifiers, rollers and seed drills were made by Fowler specifically for use with steam ploughing engines.

Steam, the power that revolutionised manufacturing and provided the impetus behind our early railways, became a force to be reckoned with on our farms in the 1860s. The centuries old combination of man and beast working the land in rustic harmony was dramatically challenged by the coming of the mighty steam ploughing engine.

Small portable steam engines towed by horses from one location to the next had been used on farms for threshing, grinding and sawing since the early part of the nineteenth century. Agricultural engineering companies were springing up around the country, particularly in the eastern counties. In Yorkshire, Leeds had become a leading centre for steam locomotive production; precisely the right working environment for the establishment in 1862 of the Steam Plough Works, founded by John Fowler, one of the nation's greatest engineers.

Born to a Quaker merchant family in Melksham, Wiltshire, in 1826,

Ready for battle: Napoleon, *a class B4 ploughing engine built by John Fowler of Leeds in 1912, poses proudly with his ploughing team; all employees of A.T. Oliver & Sons of Wandon End, Luton, Bedfordshire. The steel rope links a plough or cultivator to an identical engine,* Wellington *on the opposite side of the field.*

Steam plough teams, working mostly for contractors, usually included a foreman, two engine drivers, a ploughman and a labourer/cook. Travelling between farms, a cavalcade of two engines, living van and the necessary cultivating equipment would have been an impressive sight.

John Fowler's quest to become an engineer led him to Middlesbrough, where, at the age of twenty-one, he joined the engineering company of Gilkes, Wilson, Hopkins & Co. During a visit to Ireland in 1849 Fowler witnessed the deprivation brought upon its people by the failure of the potato crop. Deeply moved by what he saw, he resolved to direct his engineering skills towards improving farming methods and production.

Initially his efforts were concentrated on land drainage, using portable steam engines before moving on to explore the possibilities of ploughing by steam. Fowler's first self-moving steam plough (with an engine made by Clayton & Shuttleworth of Lincoln), appeared in 1857.

Slung beneath the boiler of a steam ploughing engine is a massive drum of steel cable. This is attached to a specially designed double-ended plough balanced like a see-saw on its centrally positioned wheels and axle. Early steam ploughing engines worked singly; hauling the plough backwards and forwards with the aid of a self-propelled anchor on the opposite side of the field to the engine.

John Fowler established his famous Steam Plough Works in Hunslet, Leeds, to manufacture both engines and ploughing equipment. The more efficient double-engine system of ploughing was pioneered at this time. Two engines were positioned at opposite sides of the field, winding the plough back and forth between them whilst slowly moving up the field

ABOVE, LEFT: Deserted during the Christmas break of 1919, the crowded erecting shop at John Fowler's Steam Plough works, Hunslet, Leeds, appears to indicate a healthy order book.

ABOVE, RIGHT: The dedication of hard working 'hands-on' enthusiasts has ensured that examples of every member of the traction engine family can now be seen and heard at rallies throughout the country. Renown, a Fowler showman's road locomotive built in 1920 for the showman John Murphy of County Durham is currently owned by the Howard Brothers of Kirk Ireton, Derbyshire. This magnificent engine was photographed at the 2005 Pickering Traction Engine Rally generating power for Frank Lythgoe's gallopers.

In 2003, a devastating workshop fire almost destroyed Renown. Undaunted, the Howard brothers completely re-built the engine in sixteen months.

OPPOSITE PAGE, TOP: A wonderfully evocative scene from August 1935 at Staincliffe Hall Farm near Dewsbury. Built in 1899, a McLaren traction engine provides the power for a threshing machine.

OPPOSITE PAGE, BELOW: 1928, and the pungent smell of hot tar hangs over a street in Conisbrough, South Yorkshire. Making a good deal less smoke than the vintage tar boiler in the background, a Fowler 10 ton steam roller, its rear wheels chocked against the gradient, awaits the next call to duty.

after each traverse of the plough or harrow. After each pass, the men riding the plough would dismount and tip the plough to bring the other set of shares or discs into action for its return.

In 1864, John Fowler's brother Robert became a partner in the firm. Sadly, later that year John Fowler died following a riding accident. However, John Fowler & Company (Leeds) Ltd. went on to become a world leader in steam ploughing engines and equipment, exporting throughout the world to a long list of countries that include Germany, Russia, South Africa and Australia.

Long before the internal combustion engine made its indelible mark on society, engineers were applying steam power to self-propelled agricultural and road vehicles. The horse drawn portable agricultural steam engine morphed into the steam traction engine. Forever associated with the job of threshing on farms, traction engines were also champions of road haulage, often handling loads in excess of 100 tons.

Steam ploughing engines – part of the same family tree – are impressive in a rugged, workmanlike way; but without a doubt the most visually imposing steam road vehicles ever built were the showman's road engines. Richly decorated, these powerful machines hauled lengthy convoys of fairground rides and living caravans from venue to venue, before powering-up their on-board dynamos to bring a fairground to life.

Roadworks, the bane of our lives, were at least more interesting when graced by the presence of a steamroller – another member of the traction engine family and a machine used by some local authorities into the mid 1960s.

Such was the depth of Leeds' engineering prowess that – apart from Fowler's – the city gave rise to two other companies in this field: J.H. McLaren Ltd. and Thomas Green & Sons Ltd.

The days when steam power made an ongoing contribution to farming, fairgrounds and road transport are long gone; but through the dedication of a few, working steam engines and steam fairs enable thousands to experience the sensory attractions of this evocative and 'atmospheric' form of power.

PULLING POWER IN HUNTING PINK

The machinery driving Yorkshire's thriving textile industry would have been decidedly ineffective without the ability of gear wheels to convert and fine-tune the raw power generated by water, steam or electricity.

Working from a stable in a back street in Huddersfield in 1860, David Brown began making wooden patterns from which gear wheels, principally for the local textile industry, could be cast. From these humble beginnings evolved a family concern with an unrivalled world-wide reputation for the manufacture of power transmission equipment.

Tractors have become an integral part of farming since Henry Ford introduced his mass-produced Model F in 1917. In Northern Ireland, agricultural engineer Harry Ferguson had taken time-out from repairing

tractors and agricultural machinery to develop an effective hydraulic linkage between tractor and plough. His search for a company to mass produce not only the patent linkage, but a purpose-built tractor to go with it, was resolved in 1936 when he met David Brown, grandson of the founder of David Brown & Company.

This collaboration produced the Ferguson-Brown tractor, the first in the world to be fitted with a hydraulic lift and three-point linkage, allowing both tractor and plough to operate as a single unit. A converted cotton mill in Meltham, Huddersfield, became David Brown's tractor factory.

Unfortunately, the alliance, which initially showed such promise, broke down. Two strong willed and talented engineers were unable to find sufficient common ground to continue. Ferguson crossed the Atlantic to team up with Henry Ford; eventually going on to produce the well-known T20 'Little Grey Fergie' tractor.

Even before the last Ferguson-Brown tractor rolled off the production line the prototype of its successor was up and running. The VAK 1 (Vehicle Agricultural Kerosene) featured a distinctive round nose and fairing ahead of the steering wheel. The tractor's four-cylinder 35bhp ohv engine was designed and built 'in-house'. With masterly ingenuity, David Brown engineers were able to avoid infringing any Ferguson patents and retain the all-important hydraulic three-point linkage.

When consulted regarding his views on a possible colour for the new machine, David Brown produced his hunting jacket as a colour swatch. Pink – Hunting Pink to be precise!

After the Second World War, the VAK models were superseded by the 'Cropmaster' – for many, the definitive David Brown tractor and one of the most versatile machines of its day. Almost 60,000 were made before production ceased in 1954.

The company continued to manufacture tractors – albeit with a squarer, more functional outline. In 1972 the David Brown tractor division became part of the American company, Case. In 1988 tractor production ceased in Meltham, a former textile town that found lasting recognition in the world of agriculture.

A Royal Air Force David Brown tractor tows a bomb train during the Second World War for loading prior to bombing operations. (IWM CH13710).

BOTTOM LEFT: Odsal Stadium, Bradford in the 1950s when the popularity of speedway was at its height. The implement in the middle distance will be attached to the David Brown tractor prior to raking the cinder track.

BOTTOM RIGHT: Rows of David Brown 990 'Implematic' tractors (a successor to the 'Cropmaster') await despatch from the company's Meltham factory in 1963.

BELOW: The distinctive lines of the VAK series introduced in 1939 were carried forward to the David Brown 'Cropmaster' of 1947 – one of the world's 'classic' tractors.

PERCY SHAW'S EUREKA MOMENT

On a particularly foggy night in the 1930s a motorist found himself cautiously descending the Bradford – Halifax road from its summit at Queensbury. Barely able to see more than a few feet ahead of him, his concentration focused on the tramlines reflected in his car's headlights.

Fearful of a sheer drop on his right hand side he slowly inched his car forwards. Through the eerie wall of mist and darkness, there suddenly appeared two small pin-points of light emanating from a cat sitting on a fence post. Our intrepid traveller was a practical and imaginative man, in a flash an idea came to him that would contribute to safer motoring the world over.

That man was Percy Shaw; his idea would use the power of reflected light to guide motorists along dark or fogbound roads. Brilliantly simple in concept, its execution however would lead its inventor through a painstaking journey of trial and error.

Born in Boothtown, Halifax, in 1890, Percy Shaw left school at thirteen to work in a local blanket mill. A hankering to be involved in things practical and mechanical, led him through a number of jobs in textile engineering, welding, boiler and machine-tool making. Appropriately, Shaw's 'can-do' approach to life also saw him laying private roads and paths – experience that would prove invaluable in bringing his idea to fruition.

Road vehicles were becoming faster and heavier. Set into the road surface itself, the device would have to withstand the daily onslaught of traffic, from motor cycles to steam rollers. Choosing the right materials would be crucial.

Iron, a material so important in our industrial past, gave strength and

Percy Shaw OBE, established his 'Catseyes' factory alongside his home, Boothtown Mansion, Halifax, where he lived for most of his life. Despite inventing and manufacturing a product that sold by the million, possessions meant little to Percy Shaw a true 'self-made man' who lived a private and frugal life. Luxury and contentment came in the form of a Rolls-Royce Phantom and seventeen television sets playing throughout every room of his mansion.

durability for the casing. Pure crystal glass from Czechoslovakia provided the required luminosity for the lenses, entailing the development of special moulding and cutting techniques and the use of a specially designed furnace. After further trials, the lenses were seated in hard wearing, shock absorbing vulcanised rubber.

The quest was complete, apart from the problem of keeping the lenses clean. The solution brought one last touch of genius to the job by getting the weight of the vehicle itself to depress the lenses down into the casing which incorporated a built-in cleaning device. The flexible rubber surround would spring back revealing an automatically cleaned pair of lenses.

The world-wide success of the self-cleaning reflective road stud was recognised in 1965 when Percy Shaw was awarded the OBE for his services to export. Until his death in 1976, Shaw lived in Boothtown Mansion, Halifax; next door to the factory which has produced by the million a life-saving product inspired by light reflected from the eyes of an unknown cat.

One of the world's most familiar objects. On unlit major highways and isolated winding lanes, 'Catseyes' have safely guided millions of motorists throughout the world. The self-cleaning reflective road stud invented by Percy Shaw of Halifax in the 1930s is a triumph of simplicity and effectiveness.

STREAMLINED SHOWSTOPPER

Cars – seen today as an essential part of our lives – were once looked upon as a necessity by only a few. To the thousands who felt no real loss of status travelling by train, bus or tram, the offer of a lift in a car – be it an affable Morris 8 or an imperious Armstrong Siddley Sapphire – was an experience to be savoured.

The guarded optimism following the Second World War ultimately bore the fruits of a flourishing economy and high employment, delivering the privilege of car ownership to a wider public.

1945, and freed from the bonds of the war effort, Britain's car industry could return to the 'business in hand'. Exports were a priority, but most of the country's car manufacturers would have to rely on pre-war designs. A Yorkshire car maker, based in Bradford was, however, ahead of the rest and ready to announce the country's first new post-war model.

To a British public accustomed to the sight of motor cars with a somewhat sedately outlined 'sit-up-and-beg' appearance, the Jowett Javelin's streamlined shape was a real eye opener – this really did look like the future of motoring!

A salary of £500 persuaded designer Gerald Palmer to leave MG to head up Jowett's design team in Bradford. The groundbreaking outcome was the result of working to an open brief from the start. To maximise internal space, a flat-four 1486cc die-cast aluminium engine was mounted well forward. The striking bodywork built by Briggs of Doncaster incorporated a flat floor giving passengers maximum leg room.

Initially, post-war shortages of raw materials hampered production, but an enthusiastic reception from the motoring press sustained public interest in the new car. Today, a Jowett Javelin would be hard pressed to hold its own against the average family hatch-back, but in the late 1940s a top speed of 80mph was more than respectable. 'Take a good look when it passes you' became the headline in early advertisements for the car.

Yorkshire rally drivers, Tommy Wise and Cuth Harrison chose a Jowett Javelin as their entry in the 1949 Monte Carlo Rally. The car performed faultlessly, winning the 1½ litre class and securing fourteenth place overall. Jowett, quick to capitalise on the result, entered a Javelin in

TOP: Britain's first all-new car after the Second World War, the Jowett Javelin made its public debut at the London Cavalcade of Motoring in 1946 heralding the future of family motoring. In pre-motorway days, a family enjoy an idyllic day out in their Jowett Javelin in this 1951 publicity photograph.

ABOVE: In complete contrast, Bob Foster and George Holdsworth battle through a blizzard in their Jowett Javelin on their way to thirty-seventh place in the 1952 Monte Carlo Rally.

the 24 hour race at Spa in Belgium, securing once more a successful class-winning result. Throughout the fifties Jowett Javelins turned in creditable performances in the Monte Carlo and other European rallies.

The Javelin's sporting successes paved the way for an even more impressive looking car from Jowett. With a chassis designed by ERA, one of Britain's leading racing car specialists, the Jowett Jupiter was a thoroughbred sportscar from the ground up. The car's styling, which even today elicits gasps of admiration, was the work of Jowett's chief stylist Reg Korner.

With supreme confidence, Jowett entered an early production example in the 1950 Le Mans 24 hour race. Driven by Tommy Wise and Tommy Wisdom, the Jupiter covered over eighteen hundred miles at a record average speed of 75.8 mph. This kind of sporting success – and there were

ABOVE: The shape of things to come? A Jowett Javelin speeds past a Leeds Corporation 'Horsfield' tramcar in a scene from the mid 1950s. Alas, the future of this once revolutionary car had already been sealed, when in 1954 Jowett went into receivership. The Leeds tramway system continued until 1959.

many – must have made Jowett Javelin and Jupiter owners feel more than a bit special.

During the first two decades of the twentieth century there were hundreds of firms in roadside workshops and factories throughout the country, trying their hand at making cars and motorcycles in an endeavour to harness the internal combustion engine to motorised transport. Sadly, a lack of funding for development work ensured that most vehicles produced in this way automatically became 'limited editions'.

RIGHT: A car park in the centre of
Bradford becomes an open-air motor
show in 1953. A fascinating 'period-
piece' from photographer C.H. Wood. In
the foreground, only a few miles from
where it was made, a Jowett Javelin
takes its place among cars from Britain
and America. European manufacturers
are notably absent and the influx of
makes from the Far East is still some way
off.

BELOW LEFT: One of Britain's most
popular commercial vehicles. The Jowett
Bradford light van, beloved by small
traders throughout the country is now a
'classic' in its own right.

BELOW RIGHT: The Jowett Javelin's
sensational streamlined looks were put in
the shade by its stable mate, the Jupiter
sports car. Beautifully restored examples
like the one shown are much admired by
enthusiasts of all marques.

The sons of a blacksmith, the Jowett brothers, Benjamin and William, set up the Jowett Motor Manufacturing Company in Bradford in 1901. When still in their twenties they built their first engine, a V-twin water-cooled unit. By 1905 they had completed a twin cylinder engine with horizontally opposed cylinders – a configuration at the heart of Jowett engines until the closure of the company in 1954.

Supported by general engineering work, car building began to expand until eventually in 1920 Jowett moved to a purpose-built factory at Idle on the outskirts of Bradford.

The Jowett range of light, open touring and saloon cars was the embodiment of 'freedom of the open road'. Car clubs were formed to foster social and competitive interaction. Jowett owners were encouraged to write to the company relating their experiences. The car became part of the family and an object of affection; as many family photo-albums now testify.

From the start Jowett produced light commercial vehicles. Re-starting vehicle production after the Second World War the company chose to produce a van as an expedient way of generating income whilst development work was being carried out on the all-new Javelin.

The new van was a simple, reliable, 'no-frills' vehicle that put the name of Yorkshire's premier wool city onto the high streets of towns and villages throughout Britain. Since the first Jowett Bradford van was produced in 1946, thousands have faithfully served shopkeepers, and small businesses. The 'Bradford' epitomized the industrious and genial nature of the small trader.

Volume car making in Yorkshire came to an end in the 1950s when mechanical and production problems began to afflict Jowett. Scores of Javelins, Jupiters and Bradford vans continued to grace Britain's roads, but in time, most made that final journey to the scrap yard. The fact that a precious few have survived can be attributed to the skill and dedication of a handful of enthusiasts. These custodians of 'motoring history in the round' remind us that looking back can give a sense of perspective and added value to what we take for granted today.

ABOVE: An evocative image from 1910, when car ownership was the privilege of the 'well-to- do'. A group of gentlemen – regulars at the Crown Hotel, Morley – are not to be denied a grand day out, courtesy of the internal combustion engine. Their solid-tyred charabanc was made by KarrierCar of Huddersfield, a company later to become well known for commercial vehicles.

BELOW: 'Repairs to Motor Cars, Delivery Vans, Lorries & Aeroplanes', the signs on the premises of 'The Motor House' car showroom, Division Street, Sheffield, reveals the close affinity between motoring and powered flight during the early part of the twentieth century.

THE CAT FROM CLECKHEATON

Every year since 1976, a group of motorcycle enthusiasts have gathered at the Commercial Hotel, Cleckheaton – a town once noted for textiles, engineering and wire drawing. The hostelry providing them with welcome refreshment stands guardian over a forgotten corner of Yorkshire's industrial landscape and the birthplace of every machine present on that day.

A chance meeting in 1904, between Joah Phelon, a Cleckheaton wire drawing gauge and die maker and Bradford born mill engineer, Richard Moore, became the catalyst in the creation of a legendary motorcycle marque.

With his former business partner Richard Rayner, who sadly died in a motor accident, Phelon had built a number of motorcycles whilst still serving the local wire industry. His meeting with Moore gave him a renewed sense of purpose.

Motorcycles were slowly emerging from their pedal powered ancestry. The name Phelon & Moore began to acquire a reputation for reliability and solid workmanship, winning medals in major long distance trials and hill climbing events. Export markets, including Mexico, China and the Commonwealth countries were pursued. Despatch riders with the Royal Flying Corps rode P & M machines behind the lines in the First World War.

By the mid 1920s there were more than a hundred manufacturers in Britain. Significant strides were being made in every aspect of design. Motorcycles became machines with a sense of purpose; reflected in the name PANTHER chosen for P & M's 555cc Sports model of 1923. The Isle of Man TT races and continuing success in competitive trials enhanced the growing reputation of this new name in motorcycling.

Advertised as 'The sensation of 1933', the Red Panther was one of the most important machines ever produced by Phelon & Moore. Selling at £28.17.6 made it the cheapest 250cc in Britain. This lightweight motorcycle single-handedly hauled the company back from the abyss of the Great Depression.

Defining the 'golden era' of the British motorcycle will long be an on-going debate among owners and enthusiasts. The classic designs of the inter-war years owe everything to early pioneers like Joah Phelon and fellow Yorkshireman Alfred Angus Scott, whose highly individualistic Scott motorcycles once produced in Shipley near Bradford, now enjoy the same level of loyalty from their devotees as Panther and the rest.

The last Panther rolled off the production line in 1966, when the final chapter of a once great and prolific industry was being written. To many, British motorbikes reached their zenith in the 50s and 60s. In retrospect, whatever the reasons for their commercial demise, all rode off into a glorious sunset.

Machines built by P & M and Panther could hold their own at any time with the likes of Norton, Triumph, Matchless and BSA., not just in looks but with a voice – described as a deep, almost lazy thump of an engine beat – guaranteed to double the heart rate of motorbike lovers throughout the land, ensuring that these charismatic cats from Cleckheaton make their annual pilgrimage to the Commercial Hotel for years to come.

OPPOSITE PAGE: *Panther motorcycle enthusiasts gather at the Commercial Hotel, Cleckheaton, adjacent to the site of Phelon & Moore's motorcycle factory where all the machines present at this 2006 annual rally were made.*

LEFT: *A restored 350cc Red Panther against a backdrop of the derelict P & M works in Horncastle Street, Cleckheaton.*

BELOW: *The Isle of Man TT races have long been an important event in motorcycle racing. P & M produced bikes especially for this and other races. P & Ms works rider Arthur Warwick sits astride his specially prepared 1926 500cc machine. A sight to quicken the pulse of bikers everywhere!*

Two 'classic' Panthers from the early 1950s photographed at a recent P & M Panther rally.

TRUE COLOURS

Between the old track bed of a former Whitby to Middlesbrough railway line and the North Sea is Sandsend Ness. Here walkers on the 'scenic' Cleveland Way are confronted by a promontory completely devoid of vegetation. Imagination and credibility could be stretched to the limit to realise that these few acres of lifeless shale connect historically to the way in which colour has been brought into our lives. This miniature wasteland has become a legacy to the alum industry, once so important in the dyeing, tanning and leather industries.

Wool had been England's most important export since the twelfth century. Dyer's used alum as a mordant or fixative. Until the Reformation supplies were imported from Italy, but the discovery of alum shale outcropping at several points on the Yorkshire coast from the early 1600s proved timely, giving rise to the county's first chemical industry.

Quarrying this particular mineral brought feverish industrial activity to Boulby, Kettleness, Sandsend, Saltwick and Ravenscar in particular. Alum shale was first hacked from the quarry face before being piled into huge heaps on the quarry floor and set alight. A lengthy burning process recovered alum powder from the shale. The powder was then boiled in large pans of water to which ammonia was added in the form of urine – much of it brought by boat from London. The resulting alum crystals were then ready for shipment.

In the fourteenth century the Cistercian monks of Fountains Abbey incorporated dye vats and furnaces to provide hot water into their woolhouse. Outside the confines of monastic life dyers – also known as 'listers' – were working like spinners and weavers in cottage industry fashion.

Until the gradual introduction of synthetic dyes from the 1880s, nature provided the raw materials to the dyeing industry. Plants, trees and, in the case of cochineal, insects, were crushed or boiled, to produce the basic ingredients from which the dyer would skilfully extract vibrant reds, blues and yellows.

Plants like weld – also known also as dyer's rocket – produced a brilliant yellow dye. Red dye was extracted from the roots of the madder plant. Woad, a plant from which blue dye is obtained, has been used since prehistoric times. Some plants like dyer's greenweed (yellow) and green alkanet (red) were introduced to this country by Flemish immigrant dyers in the Middle Ages. Watermill crushing machinery extracted dye from logwood imported from South America and the West Indies.

Though Flemish dyers brought their expertise to Yorkshire there was still a substantial amount of cloth exported to Antwerp for dyeing and finishing. However, by the sixteenth century, Leeds, York, Beverley, Wakefield and Halifax had become established as centres of Yorkshire's wool trade with a correspondingly growing reputation in dyeing and finishing.

Large mills like Samuel Lister's Manningham Mills, Bradford,

OPPOSITE PAGE, LEFT: Sandsend Ness, a bare knuckle of land, juts out into the North Sea a few miles north of Whitby. Between the turbulent North Sea and nature's gentler side, two centuries of alum quarrying – which ceased there in the mid-nineteenth century – has left a barren landscape of lifeless shale.

OPPOSITE PAGE, RIGHT: Whitby's distinguished maritime history is founded on the River Esk. Less well known, but no less significant, were neighbouring alum quarries. A lengthy refining process produced white alum crystals, used in the textile industry as a mordant to improve the colour fastness and brightness of dyes. Frank Meadow Sutcliffe's photograph shows the now demolished Prussian Blue dye works Whitby, surrounded by trees on the right hand bank of the River Esk.

ABOVE: The modern face of Yorkshire's chemical industry, born in the seventeenth century with the discovery of alum shale on the Yorkshire coast. Built on land formerly occupied by the famous Low Moor Iron Company near Bradford, this man-made hybrid hovers between architecture and machine, its miles of pipe work mysteriously linking industrial processes to the practicalities of production. Pugnaciously standing its ground in the shadow of this giant of the chemical industry is the Morley Carr Working Men's Club – a metaphor for the way in which earning a living invariably dominates our leisure time.

ABOVE: *The madder plant* (rubia tinctorum) *from whose roots is extracted alizarine, the source of Turkey Red Dye.*

ABOVE LEFT: *Detailed notebooks and colour samples from 1845 belonging to dyer David Smith of Halifax. The glass jars contain Safflower (dried petals of dyer's thistle) and Cudbear (a mixture of lichens).*

LEFT: *Towards the end of the nineteenth century dyes derived from natural sources began to be replaced by synthetic dyes, leading the way to a wider range of brilliant colours. This collection of synthetic dyes from the Society of Dyers and Colourists Colour Museum, Bradford, includes examples from Yorkshire and German dye makers.*

incorporated their own dyehouses. Specialist dyeworks were also on the increase. Covering over five acres, George Ripley's Bowling Dyeworks, Bradford, founded in 1808 had, by the 1880s, become the largest piece dyeing firm in the world.

Before science began to play a more significant part in the dyeing industry, producing the right shade of colour was achieved through years of experience. Foreman dyers were known to do their 'calculations' under a cloak of secrecy, making it easy to picture the medieval dyer as something of an alchemist. Whatever the methodology or outcome, there has always been a common bond between dyers and chemists.

Links to the chemical industry grew even stronger through the gradual introduction of synthetic dyes based on coal tar and petroleum derivatives. The abandonment of a centuries old tradition using natural dyes was at first met with some resistance, but synthetic dyes, pioneered in Europe in the 1870s were destined to revolutionize the dyeing industry.

Founded in 1830 Read Holliday and Sons, Huddersfield, began as coal tar distillers, manufacturing ammonia, washing powder, black lead and creosote. Thirty years later, colour began to flood into Holliday's urbane, monochromatic world when the company moved into dye making, eventually becoming one of Britain's leading independent dye makers. Emphasis on technical development enabled the company to continually patent 'new' colours in the face of strong competition from Europe.

The development of synthetic fibres from the 1920s resulted in a greater variety of cloths which could now be woven from traditional, synthetic and mixed fibres. To meet the needs for continual research, educational programmes were introduced.

The importance of colour in our lives influences our preferences; no more so than in the clothes we wear and the furnishings chosen for our homes. Like it or not, the media and something called 'market research' are continually focusing and framing consumer choice in the search for 'the look'. Relentlessly looking to the future, designers, dyers and colourists acknowledge the influences of past skills, technologies and styles. Above all is an appreciation of the fundamental role played by nature in our interpretation of colour and design.

TOP: 'Dye house fog', a well known phenomenon in the hot and humid atmosphere of dye houses, has cleared sufficiently for an unknown photographer to record the scene in the dyehouse at Saltaire Mills, Saltaire, on the outskirts of Bradford.

RIGHT: The conflict between nature and geology continues on the site of the disused alum quarries at Sandsend north of Whitby.

FOR ONE AND ALL

Along with its newest rival, the internet, television has, without doubt, been the biggest influence on our leisure time. Now capable of reaching a global audience, sport and entertainment have come a long way since crowds gathered in open fields to watch bare-knuckle fighting, bull-baiting, cock-fighting, horse racing or the ancient but less barbaric game of knur and spell.

In most cases authority's 'blind eye' allowed these early sports and pastimes to take place. 'Letting off steam' at these raucous and often brutal occasions would see the audience descend into a rowdy meleé of drunkenness and gambling.

The factory system became instrumental in defining the hours of work and leisure. In the nineteenth century sport gained respectability through agreed rules and better organisation.

Thousands follow Yorkshire's football, rugby and cricket teams at both amateur and professional levels. Being part of a noisy crowd on match day is the perfect way (depending on the result!) to end the working week. For some, the need to 'get away from it all' means retiring to the solitude of the riverbank, pigeon loft or garden shed.

A more studious approach to leisure time was encouraged by the spread of Mechanics' Institutes, an adult learning movement founded in Glasgow in 1823 and championed by local industrialists. The nineteenth century's fascination with matters of science and technology was reflected in the lectures and courses held at Institutions throughout the land.

Before recorded music took hold of our lives many churches and chapel choirs were capable of giving wonderfully assured performances of choral works like Handel's 'Messiah', establishing Yorkshire's great tradition in choral singing. Music competitions helped to raise standards – none more popular than those featuring brass bands. In encouraging the very highest qualities of musicianship these musical confrontations transform ordinary people into extraordinary performers.

Leisure activities are as varied as the workplace itself, providing the

OPPOSITE PAGE: *Local industry has faithfully supported many of Yorkshire's brass bands. Though now fewer in number, success in contests is still a source of pride to communities throughout the county. With high expectations of a top prize no doubt, Thornhill Colliery Prize Band take time to assemble for local photographer Fred Hartley before their departure from Dewsbury Central GNR station in 1911.*

ABOVE: *Spring sunshine on an April day in 1913 brings added warmth to what must have been an occasion tinged with nostalgia. Members of the Millbridge Working Men's Club near Heckmondwike gather for the last time before the club with its distinctive wooden facade is demolished to make way for its stone built successor. Chairs and buffets have been brought out on to the Huddersfield Road pavement. The banter preceding the standing and seating arrangements has aroused the curiosity of local children, many of whom will have fathers, grandfathers and uncles among the group of adults. The illustration is based on a photograph from Norman Ellis's wonderful postcard archive.*

means to enrich the lives of millions. Despite the material wealth of some professional organisations and participants, their success is rooted in the past endeavours of aspiring amateurs.

THIS PAGE, TOP: The game of knur and spell can be traced back to the Middle Ages. Thousands would gather to watch it being played. A small ball (the knur), is fired into the air by a spring loaded device (the spell). The player has to drive the ball as far as possible with a stick. In the Calder Valley area, knur and spell was played until the 1970s. Known in this part of Yorkshire as 'billets', the knur was held in a small sling. The photograph shows the game being played in the village of Heptonstall near Halifax in the 1960s. Contestants await their turn, hoping to beat Eric Barker's energetic attempt.

THIS PAGE, BELOW: Sheffield's industrial might personified by the tug-of-war team fielded at the turn of the twentieth century by one of the city's steel firms that eventually became Firth Brown.

OPPOSITE PAGE, TOP LEFT: Early air displays, with their heady mixture of wonder, daring, spectacle and, for some, morbid curiosity, attracted spectators from far and wide. Mr. B.C. Hucks' Bleriot monoplane awaits the next opportunity to thrill the crowd at the 1913 Barnsley Hospital Aviation Meeting.

OPPOSITE PAGE, CENTRE LEFT: For millions, church and chapel were the epicentre of social life. In the early 1920s, the women and girls of Hightown Primitive Methodist Chapel near Cleckheaton staged 'Ye Olde Village Wedding' for their Married Ladies Concert.

OPPOSITE PAGE, BELOW LEFT: In the days when holidays were few and far between, the works outing was an eagerly anticipated event. Staff of British Belting & Asbestos Ltd. Cleckheaton, prepare to board their coaches for the company's annual day trip to the coast.

OPPOSITE PAGE, RIGHT: An evocative view bird's-eye view of Walsden, a textile town on Yorkshire's western border with Lancashire. Saturday afternoon; the sun is out and smoke from the town's mills has cleared, allowing near perfect conditions for a game of cricket. Like many other small towns and villages, Walsden supported a variety of sporting and leisure activities including of course, football. Walsden United successfully lifted the impressive Calder Valley Shield in 1924.

ARNSLEY HOSPITAL AVIATION MEETING, 1913.
MR. B. C. HUCKS' BLÉRIOT MONOPLANE.

BRITISH BELTING & ASBESTOS LTD. SCANDINAVIA MILLS
PRIVATE

*150 hp low pressure steam turbine by Greenwood & Batley., Leeds — once one of Yorkshire's largest engineering concerns.
Working in every branch of mechanical engineering the company built steam engines, torpedoes for the Admiralty and machinery for a variety
of trades. Diversification into electrical engineering came during the late nineteenth century.*

AT THE FLICK OF A SWITCH

Children working the night shift at a Burley-in-Wharfedale water powered cotton mill in 1802 complained to the mill owner that they had difficulty in seeing what they were doing – they were after all working by candlelight. Most would be well into their teens before a new mill equipped with gas lighting was built in 1811 – six years after Lodge's Mill in Sowerby Bridge near Halifax became the first textile mill in Britain to be lit by gas. Other mills followed, many building their own

A spectacle visible from as far away as the North York Moors and the Pennines. On a bitterly cold day, steam from the power source of a million kettles, rises skywards to dwarf the 850ft chimney and massive cooling towers of Drax Power Station near Selby. Completed in 1986 and generating 4,000 MW, Drax, Britain's largest coal-fired power station, is fitted with Flue Gas Desulphurisation equipment to considerably reduce sulphur dioxide emissions.

plants for refining coal gas.

In a century dominated by steam power it is easy to underestimate the impact gas lighting must have made upon manufacturing and commerce.

By the 1830s town and city streets were being lit by gas supplied by private companies. Lighting was, for some years seen as the only use for gas, being at first restricted to public buildings and industry which increasingly began to utilise gas in furnaces, ovens and kilns. By the end of the nineteenth century gaslight illuminated the majority of homes. Cooking and heating by gas were luxuries only the following century would begin to provide.

At around the same time that mill workers first began to enjoy the benefits of working by gaslight, scientist Michael Faraday used coils of wire and magnets to demonstrate the principle of electromagnetism. Faraday's experiments conducted between 1821 and 1831 proved that an electric current could be turned into mechanical motion – the principle behind the electric motor – and that the mechanical motion of a copper disc rotating between the poles of a magnet generated an electric current, creating a simple generator or dynamo. Though of little practical value at the time, these simple devices laid the foundations of an entirely new

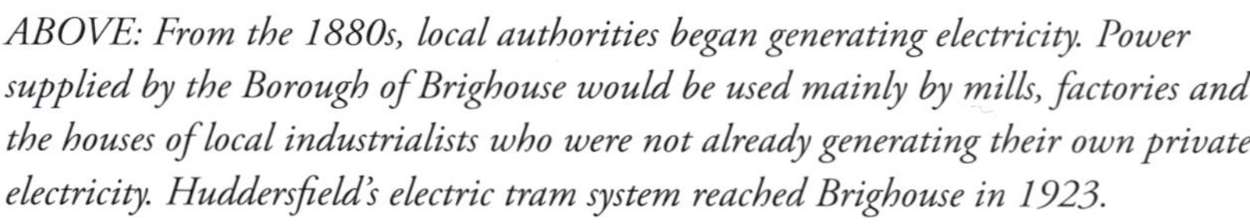

ABOVE: From the 1880s, local authorities began generating electricity. Power supplied by the Borough of Brighouse would be used mainly by mills, factories and the houses of local industrialists who were not already generating their own private electricity. Huddersfield's electric tram system reached Brighouse in 1923.

TOP RIGHT: One of Frank Meadow Sutcliffe's less well-known photographs captures workmen laying a cable at low tide under the River Esk, Whitby, in 1910.

OPPOSITE PAGE: Established in 1889, Ullathorne & Edmondson, of Bradford, were early pioneers in 'the manufacture of machinery and apparatus for electric lighting and the transmission of power, dynamos, motors, arc lamps, switches, fuses, carbons and every accessory'. Their dynamo of 1900 expresses the new visual language introduced into the world of machinery by electricity.

industry; electrical engineering.

As early as 1840, Sheffield silversmiths were suspending articles of base metals in a tank of solution. Passing an electric current through it caused silver to be deposited on the articles. Electroplating, as it became known, provided a cheaper alternative to solid silver. This technique was also used in other areas of metallurgy.

A much more dramatic use of electricity was first employed by the steel industry prior to the Second World War. Giant electric arc furnaces employing thousands of volts were used to melt iron and scrap steel. Discharging molten metal from one of these giants creates an awesome spectacle of sparks and flames.

Now an indispensable part of life, electricity made a somewhat low-key entrance into the daily lives of our forebears, making its public debut by way of limited arc light schemes in town centres. In 1878 the world's first floodlit football match was played at Bramall Lane, Sheffield, under arc lights supplied by the Sheffield Electric Light Co., who saw it as an opportunity to demonstrate this new source of power.

By the 1880s the current had begun to flow from science towards the equally fertile plains of engineering and industry. Specialist companies manufacturing lighting, dynamos and electric motors were formed. Many had electrically lit showrooms – an example being described in a journal at the time as 'replete with all the latest appliances in electrical

By the early part of the twentieth century, Britain's electric tramway system had begun to seriously threaten the future of some local railway services, but provided new business for companies diversifying into electrical engineering.

LEFT: The engine room at Crown Point Power Station, Leeds, built in 1897 to supply power to the city's expanding electric tramway system. Steam boilers were fed by water from the River Aire, on which barges brought coal to the site. Much of the equipment was supplied by Leeds manufacturers. Four horizontal steam engines totalling 800hp by John Fowler & Company were linked to dynamos made by Greenwood and Batley.

BELOW LEFT: Track laying at the junction of The Mount and Holgate Street, York in 1909 was typical of the widespread disruption created by the expansion of the electric tramways.

BELOW RIGHT: The trolley bus provided another form of electrically powered public transport pioneered in Bradford and Leeds in 1911. A 'trackless', as they were known locally, poses beside a centuries old form of commercial haulage in the Laisterdyke area of Bradford.

fittings, suitable either for the drawing room of a mansion or the largest mill'.

Steam power made a monumental contribution to electricity's eventual domination of daily life, with the invention of the steam turbine by Charles Parsons in 1884. High speed steam pushing steel blades in a circular motion – rather than the forwards and backwards movement of a piston in a cylinder – provides a faster, smoother continuous delivery of power. Linked to generators, steam turbines are still at the heart of our power stations today.

Electricity slowly began to make its mark on the workplace, but would reach a much wider audience by transforming horse-drawn and steam tramway systems established in towns throughout the country. Michael Holroyd Smith and Louis Crossley, electrical engineers from Halifax, were instrumental in Blackpool's decision to build an experimental electric tram line in 1885. After conducting its own trials, Leeds became the first municipality in Yorkshire to operate electric tramcars in 1897 signalling the end of horse and steam powered public transport on Britain's roads.

During the first decade of the twentieth century, hundreds of miles of track and overhead wiring were constructed. For the first time the power of electricity came into the daily lives of a population whose creature comforts at home still revolved around coal fires and gas light.

Electric tramways required power stations and generating equipment, presenting new opportunities for engineering companies like Greenwood & Batley and John Fowler of Leeds who, having recognised the future of this new power, began to design and build equipment for a variety of applications including the mining industry, where for example, Carlton Main Colliery Co. in South Yorkshire built a 10,000 volt power station at Frickley Colliery in 1906. From this, power was supplied to a number of other mines and local villages in the area.

The introduction of the electric motor into manufacturing is a much overlooked chapter in our industrial history. Founded in 1904, Brook Motors of Huddersfield became a world leader in this particular field exporting to over 60 countries and producing units from 1/6 hp up to 650 hp. Compact, clean and powerful, electric motors changed the face of manufacturing – none more so than in the textile industry.

Becks Mill, Keighley, was the first mill to be powered by electricity, with machinery driven by an electric motor positioned on each floor. In time, machinery became individually linked to its own electric motor. In a steady transition, miles of overhead shafts and belting, and the stationary steam engines from which they transmitted power, were consigned to

ABOVE: Carpet manufacturer, Louis J. Crossley's fascination with science and electricity led him to build a laboratory and workshop at his home 'Moorside', Halifax. Several dynamos powered electric lighting, an organ and a miniature electric tramway in the garden.

BELOW: Featuring a mixed programme of variety acts and short silent films, the grandly named Royal Electric Theatre, Hebden Bridge, photographed in 1913, would have been using electricity to power its projector and lighting. Some places of entertainment at this time, employed gas engines to drive electric generators.

history, resulting in a safer, much less cluttered working environment. The mills themselves began to install plant to generate electricity on site.

The domestic light bulb, jointly credited to Joseph Swan and Thomas Edison, enabled electricity to cross the threshold of everyday life. Like gas before it, industry and commerce had staked their claim on electricity some time before its flick-of-a-switch benefits could be appreciated in the majority of homes.

The 1920s saw the spread of 'ideal home' tree-lined suburbia, creating a new, cleaner, living environment where the matchless fume-free power of electricity would begin to slowly revolutionise the way we live.

Electricity – a source of intrigue to those who first encountered it – leapt across the twin terminals of science and commerce to create a major new industry; electrical engineering. Michael Faraday who died in 1867, may well have anticipated the impact electricity would have on the then industrially developing world; but its intrinsic contribution and the diversity of its application in the technological revolution we take for granted, would surely have astounded him.

ABOVE: The interior of the roving department in a Bradford mill showing the complex arrangement of line shafting and belts. Fitting electric motors to each machine made the working environment in mills quieter, safer and more open.

RIGHT: The ADA 'Coronation' power wringer and washing machine, manufactured in 1953 by Ajax Appliances of Halifax whose origins were in machine tool making. Only after World War II did such labour saving devices begin to have an impact on the domestic lives of most families in Britain.

OPPOSITE PAGE: A couple of sizeable spanners leaning against consoles displaying an array of dials, bring meaning to the term 'electrical engineering' in the power generation room of Manningham Mills, Bradford. The room originally housed a 2,000 hp steam engine prior to the change to steam turbines in the 1930s. Photographed by Tim Smith shortly before decommissioning in 1989.

Nº 2 TURBINE
Nº 1 TURBINE
STEAM
BOILER HOUSE
METERS
VELVET WEAVING, FINISHING, ETC.

CRAFTSMAN'S ART AND MUSIC'S MEASURE

John Laycock 1808-1889. Handloom weaver turned organ builder.

TOP: One of his most important commissions was to build an organ for Bolton Abbey in 1880.

RIGHT: A miniature in stone of the first organ built by John Laycock adorns his grave in the churchyard at Kildwick.

Hidden away in a secluded corner of the graveyard of Kildwick parish church, midway between Keighley and Skipton, can be found a small but arresting monument to one of Yorkshire's master-craftsmen of music. A stone-carved miniature of a chapel organ, marks the grave of John Laycock, whose skill as an organ builder brought the hymns of Charles Wesley, Isaac Watts and others to congregations across Yorkshire and Lancashire.

Appropriately, hills and moorland were never far away from the many churches and chapels blessed with the fruits of John Laycock's labours. After all, this man, born in Glusburn in 1808, began his working life as a handloom weaver, following in the footsteps of generations of his family before him. The repetitive operation of the handloom held little sway with Laycock, whose aspirations yearned for things mechanical and scientific.

A step in the right direction came when he began an apprenticeship as a wheelwright with his uncle George. An adeptness to work in both wood and metal brought the building and repairing of farm machinery to the workshop of the wheelwright. This mastery of a wide range of skills enabled John Laycock to turn his hand to almost any task; including repairs to looms, pianos and clocks, and the making of coffins. Repair work to a small number of organs also came his way.

Having played the flute in a local band, John Laycock's love of music must have influenced the purchase for £5 of a redundant organ from a local chapel. Any musical tendencies though were soon stifled by his analytical and practical faculties. The decision to build something as good, if not better, completely changed the direction John Laycock's life.

The year 1840 marked Laycock's transition from wheelwright to organ builder. The Wesleyan Chapel at Crosshills became the first recipient of an instrument by John Laycock. Initially business was slow to build up, but his carpentry skills and the repair and tuning of existing organs kept him and his family solvent.

By the 1870s brass plaques bearing the legend 'John Laycock Organ Builder', could be found on new instruments throughout Yorkshire

One of Arkengarthdale's hidden gems. An organ by John Laycock can still be seen and heard in Langthwaite Methodist Church. The instrument was sent by rail from Laycock's organ works at Crosshills to Richmond. The remaining twenty mile journey to Langthwaite was accomplished by a cavalcade of farm carts pulled by teams of shire horses. Large crowds gathered en-route to witness what turned out to be a memorable event.

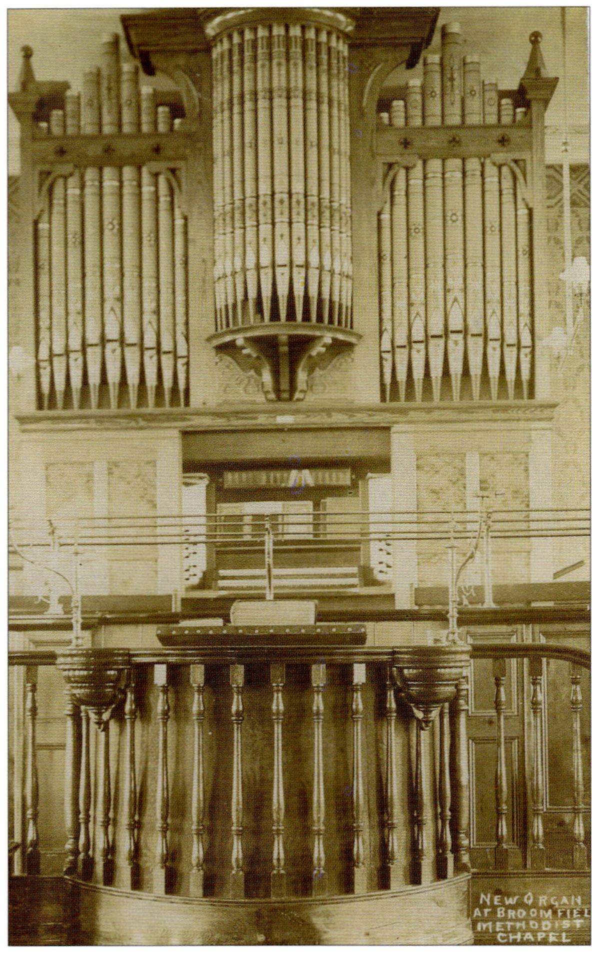

and Lancashire; ranging in size from the small single keyboard type to larger examples like the organ with three manuals built for the Wesleyan Chapel, Leeds, costing £392.

John Laycock died in 1889, and the business passed into the hands of his son William and Laycock's foreman Charles Bannister. As Laycock & Bannister the firm continued the work of its founder, moving into the era when hand and hydraulically powered organ bellows were being replaced by electric motors. In the years prior to the Second World War, the company began to introduce electro-pneumatic technology into their consoles, enabling the keyboard to be sited away from the main organ casing and pipe work.

The origins of the organ can be traced back to Greek and Roman times. Small organs with hand pumped bellows began to appear in England in the sixteenth century. By the seventeenth century Puritanism brought about the widespread destruction of the instrument throughout the country. The Restoration became a turning point, when once again the organ was allowed to contribute to worship through musical expression. Nevertheless, organs were not to be found in every church, where small orchestras were the preference of some congregations.

The expansion of Nonconformity in the nineteenth century marked the great era of chapel building. By the 1870s there were over twenty organ builders in the West Riding of Yorkshire, where the names of Isaac Abbot (later Abbot and Smith) of Leeds, Driver & Haigh and Thomas Hughes of Bradford, Kirkland and Booth, Wakefield, Peter Conacher, Huddersfield and Brindley and Foster of Sheffield, joined John Laycock and others to build organs for churches and chapels throughout Yorkshire and beyond.

The ebb and flow of social change usually means progress in one

direction and decline in another. By the 1960s church and chapel attendance was well past its high water mark, bringing closure and demolition to thousands of ecclesiastical buildings. Though some organs were rescued – most, because they were an integral part of the fabric of a building – met their end in the dust and rubble of demolition. With centuries of history behind it the 'King of Instruments' found itself in a changing world.

Electronics have been used in organ building for decades, but traditional carpentry skills, and the role of the 'voicer' – one who gives an organ its individual sound – remain as important as ever.

In making the transition from weaver to organ builder, John Laycock added his own contribution to the illustrious archives of an instrument whose presence brings resonance to the soaring stonework and stained glass of a cathedral, or stirs the soul within the confines of a remote moorland chapel.

OPPOSITE PAGE, LEFT: A rear view of the former Bolton Brow Wesleyan Chapel, Sowerby Bridge, built in 1832. In 1897 the bellows supplying wind to the chapel's organ were converted to hydraulic power, drawing water from the adjacent Calder & Hebble Navigation Canal.

OPPOSITE PAGE, RIGHT: A commemorative postcard published by a local photographer, showing the new organ built by Thomas Hughes of Bradford for Broomfield Methodist Church, Cleckheaton.

ABOVE LEFT: Design proposals by well known Huddersfield organ builders, Peter Conacher & Co., Ltd. The drawing shows the organ casing intended for Middlewich Parish Church, Cheshire.

ABOVE RIGHT: Timber, the principle material in organ building, is well in evidence in this interior view of Conacher's organ works, Huddersfield, in 1992. Established in 1854 the company were principally church organ builders who also built a number of organs for theatres and cinemas.

'DISTINCTLY A GENIUS'

A round cherubic portrait of the moon and four mid-nineteenth century ladies representing the four seasons, provide a colourfully rich pictorial narrative to the face of a longcase clock in Shibden Hall Museum, Halifax.

Saddleworth church is also featured; this Pennine town on the Lancashire-Yorkshire border being the birthplace in 1812, of the clock's creator, Samuel Broadbent Pinchin.

S.B. PINCHIN – GREETLAND is clearly lettered across the centre of the dial, but intriguingly, the story behind this fine example of the clockmaker's art reveals that it was most likely to have been made three miles away in Brighouse.

Clockmaking must have presented a challenge to Samuel Broadbent Pinchin, who began his working life in the mechanics shop of a Saddleworth mill. His 'natural abilities' enabled him to acquire the necessary skills as an engineer without the benefit of an apprenticeship. His fellow engineers threatened strike action unless Pinchin was dismissed. His employer's view that he was 'the best man in the shop' stood for nothing and Pinchin had to move on, finding employment at a mill in Greetland.

1847 found him living in Brighouse and working in the mechanics shop at Mill Royd Mill. Although no exact dates are recorded, it is thought that Pinchin's clock dates from around this time.

Undeniably a capable engineer, Pinchin was also an accomplished carpenter, enabling him in his spare time to produce examples of domestic furniture. Combine this sphere of craftsmanship with mathematical dexterity and technical ingenuity, and the true art of the clockmaker can be appreciated.

Even before he began work on the clock, Pinchin made a wheel-cutting engine to accurately fashion the clock's gears. The 5-day movement incorporates a set of bells that can be pre-set by a dial on the clock's face to play any one of six hymn tunes every three hours. The month and date are also displayed.

The painted rolling moon dial – a feature on many longcase clocks since the mid eighteenth century – moves in an arc, recording the 29½-day lunar cycle.

In the 1850s, Samuel Broadbent Pinchin, a mechanic at a Brighouse cotton mill, spent seven years designing and constructing a 5-day longcase clock. Behind its richly painted dial is a movement that enabled the clock to display the time, date, and lunar cycle. Six hymn tunes could be played by the clock's chiming mechanism.

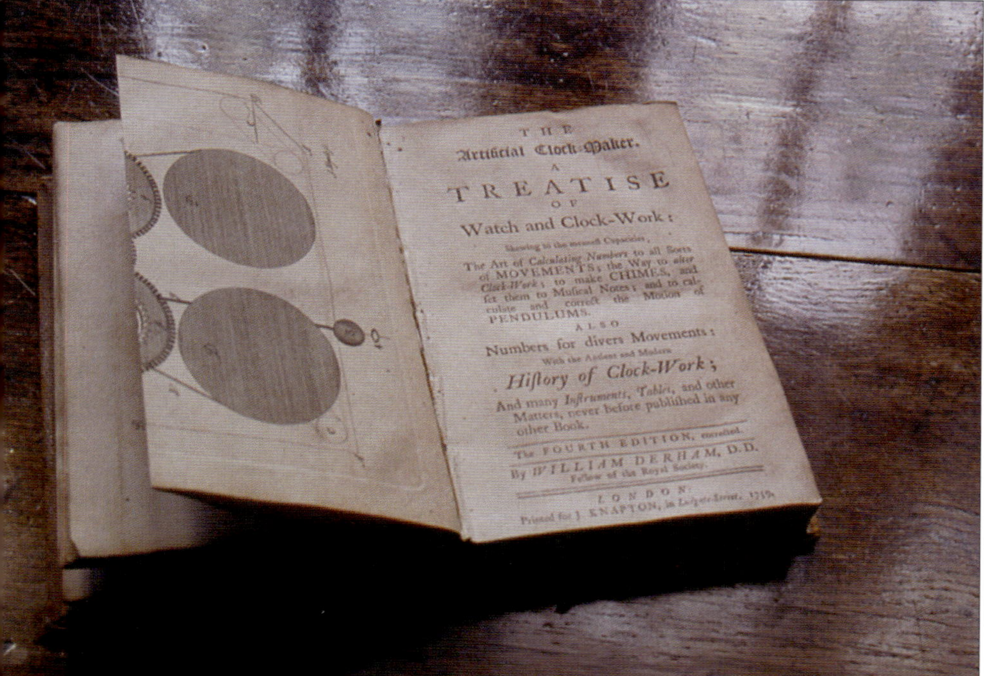

In nearby Halifax, which along with York, Leeds, Hull, Sheffield and Pontefract became a centre of clockmaking in the eighteenth century, some makers were incorporating their own type of moon dial in their clocks. The monthly passing of the moon on the dial of a Halifax Moon Clock, can be observed through a cut-out hole about the size of an old penny.

Towns and villages in and around the Pennine hills of the Calder Valley, west of Halifax, were home to a number of clockmakers. Here and elsewhere in Yorkshire, the skills of clockmaking were often handed down through successive generations.

James Ogden (1640-1735) was a yeoman of Soyland and one of four brothers, who between them founded a complex family tree of clockmakers that eventually spread from Sheffield to Bainbridge in Wensleydale and beyond to Newcastle.

Clockmaking in Halifax is synonymous with the Lister family, although Keighley was the birthplace of William Lister I in 1715. Sons of William, Thomas I and William II continued their father's trade; William working in Keighley, whilst Thomas moved to Luddenden, where he became apprenticed to John Stancliffe, the head of another distinguished

Tho Lister
HALIFAX

clockmaking family. Thomas Lister II continued the Lister line, initially working with his father before moving to Halifax.

Clockmaking became widespread throughout Yorkshire, being practiced by both individual craftsmen and makers employing several workmen. In both instances there were examples of makers using readymade components in the assembly of clocks. Dials were often made by specialist engravers, and cases by outside carpenters – factors that occasionally baffle and intrigue present day collectors.

Of the thousands built we are fortunate that so many wonderful timepieces have survived – each its own marker across a wide spectrum of craftsmanship; from the comparatively prosaic, to examples of startling ingenuity like the astronomical and world-time dialled clocks.

Samuel Broadbent Pinchin died in 1872. His clock, which took seven years to make, remains the only example ever made by this ordinary but remarkable man. In the opinion of the late S.H. Hamer a member of the Halifax Antiquarian Society; 'S.B. Pinchin was distinctly a genius, and one whose name should be put on record.'

OPPOSITE PAGE, TOP LEFT: Mill Royd Mill, a former cotton mill in Brighouse where S.B. Pinchin worked as a mechanic.

OPPOSITE PAGE, TOP RIGHT: The 5-day movement of Pinchin's long-case clock showing the set of bells and hammers enabling it to play six hymn tunes.

OPPOSITE PAGE, BELOW: A Treatise of Watch and Clock-Work by William Derham, D.D. Published in 1759 this copy belonged to Halifax clockmaker Thomas Lister II.

THIS PAGE, LEFT: The signature engraved on the dial of a long-case clock by Thomas Lister II (1745-1814).

CENTRE: Thirty-hour clock with carved oak case made about 1760 by John Stancliffe of Barkisland. The clock features a Halifax Moon located in the centre of the dial below the XII.

ABOVE: The moors above Luddenden. A number of Halifax clockmakers lived and worked in the remote towns and villages of the Calder Valley.

Hartshead St Peter near Brighouse. The winter of 1991 provides a tough test for the clock made and installed by William Potts & Sons Ltd., Leeds in 1912.

FAMILIAR FACES

Back in the days when few people regularly wore a pocket or wrist watch, the clocks on churches, town halls, railway stations, libraries and mills, helped the population at large to keep track of time. Even if you can't see them, the friendly, sonorous chimes of our public clocks can be heard across the countryside or above the cacophony of town and city life.

Working in all weathers they are often taken for granted. Seeing a public clock 'out-of-action', its hands frozen by a mechanical defect, or worse still, by terminal decline, can bring on momentary feelings of incredulity and disappointment.

Compared to the number of domestic clockmakers, manufacturers of public or turret clocks – so called because of their location in turrets or towers – are much fewer in number. Of these, one name stands way above the rest: Potts of Leeds.

At 11.15 a.m. on Friday August 18th 1961, fire broke out at Albert Mills in the centre of Morley near Leeds. The building, then in use as a paper store, became an inferno within minutes.

Like an angry mob, burning embers spiralling skywards began to attack the dome and clock tower of Morley's Town Hall a few yards away from the conflagration. Within minutes, the town's most prominent landmark had become a flaming beacon as flames took hold of the dome's internal timber framework.

The clock mechanism, installed by Potts of Leeds in 1895, continued

Friday August 18th 1961 and time is ticking away for the doomed clock mechanism in the tower of Morley Town Hall. Within minutes the wooden framework of the dome will yield to the burning embers from a nearby mill fire, and the clock, installed by William Potts & Sons, Leeds, in 1895 will be destroyed.

Made in 1848, the turret clock in All Saints Parish Church, Ilkley, is the earliest known working example by renowned Yorkshire clockmaker William Potts of Pudsey. The mechanism was designed by distinguished lawyer and amateur horologist Edmund Beckett Denison, who declared: 'I believe a clock made in this way will go as well as it is possible for a turret clock to go.'

to steadfastly count the minutes to its eventual destruction, which came at 11.30 a.m. Firemen ran for their lives as timber and masonry 'crashed down the tower like a cannonade exploding', heralding a violent end to a piece of precision engineering and a faithful sixty-six-year old servant of the town.

William Potts was born in 1809, the son of a Darlington clockmaker, and moved to Pudsey near Leeds in 1833, setting up as a clock and watchmaker. By 1840 he had begun making turret clocks for local mills. He may well have continued to become just another Yorkshire clockmaker had he not in 1847, competed for the order of a new clock for All Saints' Parish Church, Ilkley.

The interview panel included Edmund Beckett Denison, distinguished lawyer, mathematician and amateur horologist. William Potts' positive responses to questions relating to the clock impressed Denison enough to win the contract.

For William Potts, Edmund Denison's involvement with what is now the oldest working Potts turret clock, went beyond that first handshake of approval. Completed in 1848 the clock is based on Denison's design and specification, a collaboration which founded a lifelong association of shared mutual respect.

Orders for new clocks and the maintenance of existing turret clocks began to arrive. In 1865, Potts became official clockmakers to the Great Northern Railway. The name and reputation of Potts of Leeds had begun its own journey to national and international recognition.

Throughout the nineteenth century, Britain's manufacturing pre-eminence was changing the face of her towns and cities. Town halls, some rivalling the great churches and cathedrals in size, were being built. City centre streets were lined with offices, shops, arcades and department stores. The railways announced their arrival through impressive hotels and termini. Schools, hospitals and libraries became enveloped in the transformation.

Whatever their architectural style or function, one external feature brought a singleness of purpose to many of these buildings. Incorporating a clock face into the facade of a building makes it more memorable. The associations of accurate timekeeping with an organisation's worthiness

Thousands will have noted the time whilst hurrying through the impressive gateway to Bowling Mills Combing Company, Bradford. Above their heads, the mechanism by Bradford clockmaker James Shaw Son & Co. will only have been seen by a handful during its lifetime.

LEFT: Installed by William Potts & Sons, Leeds, in 1904, the clock on the library and public baths, York Road, Leeds, was, by the 1970s looking sadly neglected. It has since been fully restored.

ABOVE: One of Yorkshire's most memorable public clocks can be seen in Thornton's Arcade, Leeds. To the delight of generations of children and adults, four life-size automaton figures by Leeds sculptor J.W. Appleyard, strike the hour and quarter chimes. The characters are from Sir Walter Scott's Ivanhoe. The clock by William Potts & Sons, Leeds, was installed in 1877.

OPPOSITE PAGE, LEFT: A Bradford landmark gone forever. St James' Wholesale Market in the Eastbrook area of the city was demolished in the 1970s along with its Potts clock of 1879.

OPPOSITE PAGE, RIGHT: Municipal magnificence! Opened in 1863, Sir Charles Barry's recently restored Town Hall, Halifax, provides the ultimate setting for a public clock. The clock's original mechanism by an unknown maker was replaced by Potts in 1922.

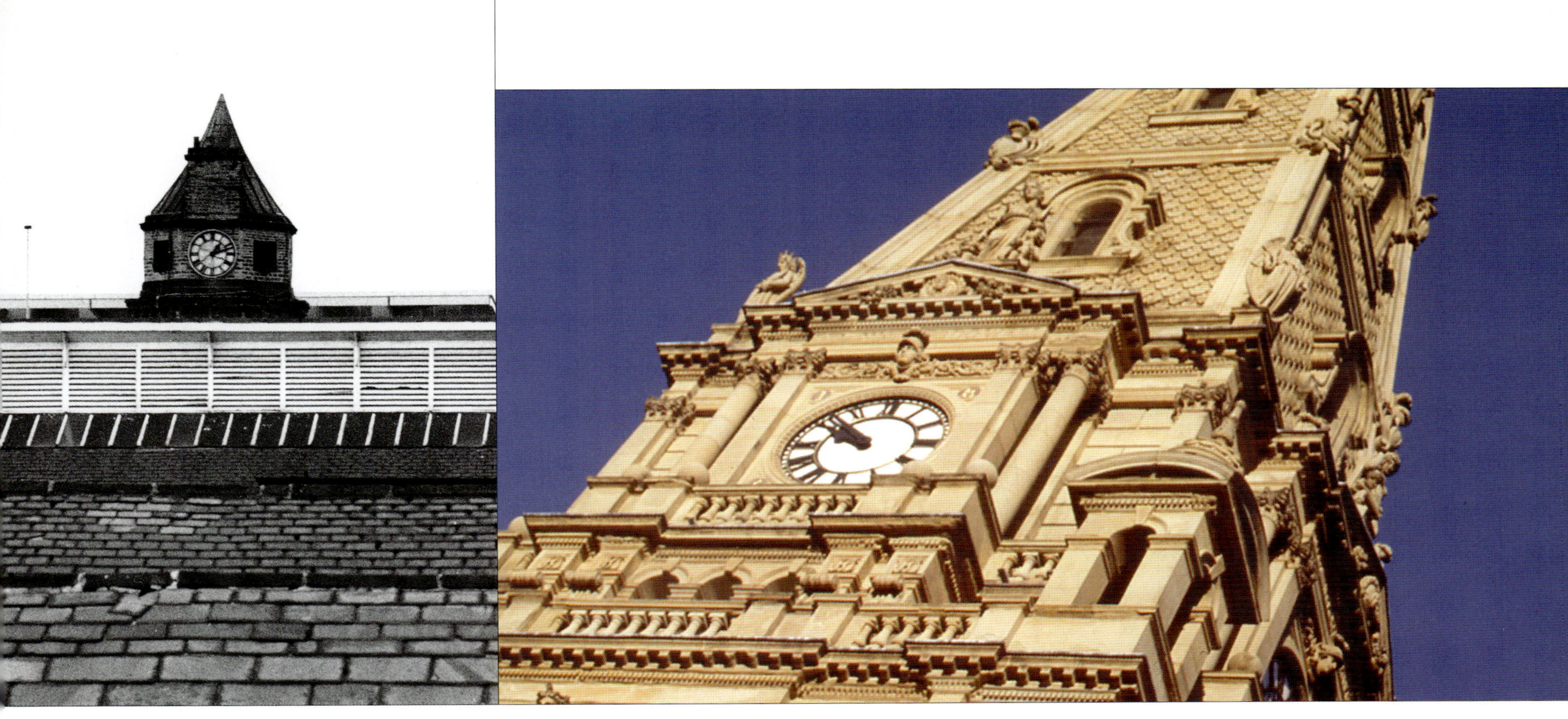

and reliability were borne by turret clockmakers like Potts of Leeds.

Turret clock making was at its height during the latter half of the nineteenth century. Three of William Potts' four sons became partners in the company. Their experience was subsequently passed on to later generations of the family.

Throughout Britain the scale and diversity of work undertaken by Potts was impressive; from lofty cathedrals and humble churches and chapels to clocks for public buildings, both grandiose and paternal. Public clocks became permanent symbols of celebration. Hundreds were built to mark the Golden and Diamond Jubilees of Queen Victoria in 1887 and 1897.

Potts became yet another Yorkshire company to establish a world-wide presence. In 1859 a clock was exported to Argentina. Others would follow to grace buildings and public squares in Russia, Afghanistan and throughout what was then the British Empire.

The expansion of towns and cities eventually ran its course and the years leading up to the Great War saw a fluctuation in the fortunes of public clockmakers; Potts being no exception.

Since the eighteenth century, clock making in all its forms has coursed through the heart of the Potts family. Despite a series of boardroom rifts, the name 'Potts' continued its association with clock making until the 1960s, when the last new clock supplied by Charles H. Potts & Co., marked the end of the family's outstanding contribution to horology and public life.

GONE, BUT NOT FORGOTTEN . . .

Amongst scores of others, the graves of two cordwainers can be found in the churchyard of Halifax Minster. Almost two centuries of wind and rain have almost obliterated the once sharply incised letters carved in stone, taking with them a word that has all but disappeared from common use. Today, 'shoemaker' would describe the profession of Thomas Gledhill 1783-1838 and James Schofield 1753-1825.

Churchyards, burial grounds and cemeteries are silent gazetteers of social history. Here documentation set in stone has created a concise and enduring record of lives – some brief in themselves – many of which have survived for centuries.

BELOW: Yeomen and cloth merchants are interred in the churchyard of Batley All Saints. An engineer, mason, tanner, butcher and the wife of a skinner are also buried here, in a town well-known for the rag and shoddy wool trade.

The abundant richness and variety of past working life can be garnered from these stone archives, where individuals whose trades and professions were valued enough in the community and fittingly recognised when the time came to commemorate their passing.

Fittingly, the lives of woolstaplers, cloth dressers, skinners, tanners, stay makers, butchers, brush makers, master mariners and Collectors of Excise have been indebted to the skills of the stonemason to provide a lasting memorial to their own talents.

For the majority, whose occupations are not recognised at the scene of their last resting place, their surnames are often derived from their place of origin or involvement in past occupations. Among the most obvious are Carpenter, Taylor, Miller, and Collier; and those whose surnames have, over time, become less apparent: Barker (Tanner), Jagger (Carrier), Webster (Weaver), Walker (Fuller), Smith (Blacksmith), and Lister (Dyer).

Mechanisation, mass-production and a more mobile workforce have transformed the working landscape of Britain in every way. Communities are no longer fully dependent upon local trades and craftsmen, whose sons and daughters served their apprenticeships within walking distance of their own homes.

A walk around a graveyard need not be a too sombre an experience. Their attributes and delights may not be revealed in an instant, but patience will eventually be rewarded, and you might be tempted to ask yourself, as I did – what exactly was a cordwainer? At some time in the future, in the same situation, will we ponder when we see the words 'computer programmer' staring back at us?

Mr. Jonathan Castlehow, no less. A simple token of respect bestowed upon an eighteenth century woolstapler, whose grave can be found in the burial ground of Halifax Minster. For centuries wool was of prime importance to the local economy in the Pennines. 'Staple' refers to the fibres of wool eg: long, short, coarse or fine. Woolstaplers, whose profession was held in high regard, were responsible for grading and classifying wool between producers and manufacturers. The stone's carved lettering features the curious use of the letter 'f' indicating a long sounding pronunciation of the letter 's'.

TOP LEFT: IN MEMORY OF
ANTHONY NELSON of Halifax
CORN DEALER
who departed this Life, on the 31st day of January 1832
Aged 39 Years. HALIFAX MINSTER

LOWER LEFT:
HERE RESETH THE BODY OF
RICHARD WILLAN, late
SUPERVISOR OF EXCISE
in Halifax who departed this life September 18th 1797
Aged 54 Years. HALIFAX MINSTER

LOWER RIGHT:
SACRED TO THE MEMORY OF
MARY TALBOT, the wife of JAMES TALBOT of this
Town, **SKINNER**
who departed this life on the 17th day of July 1820
in the 59th Year of her age. BATLEY, ALL SAINTS

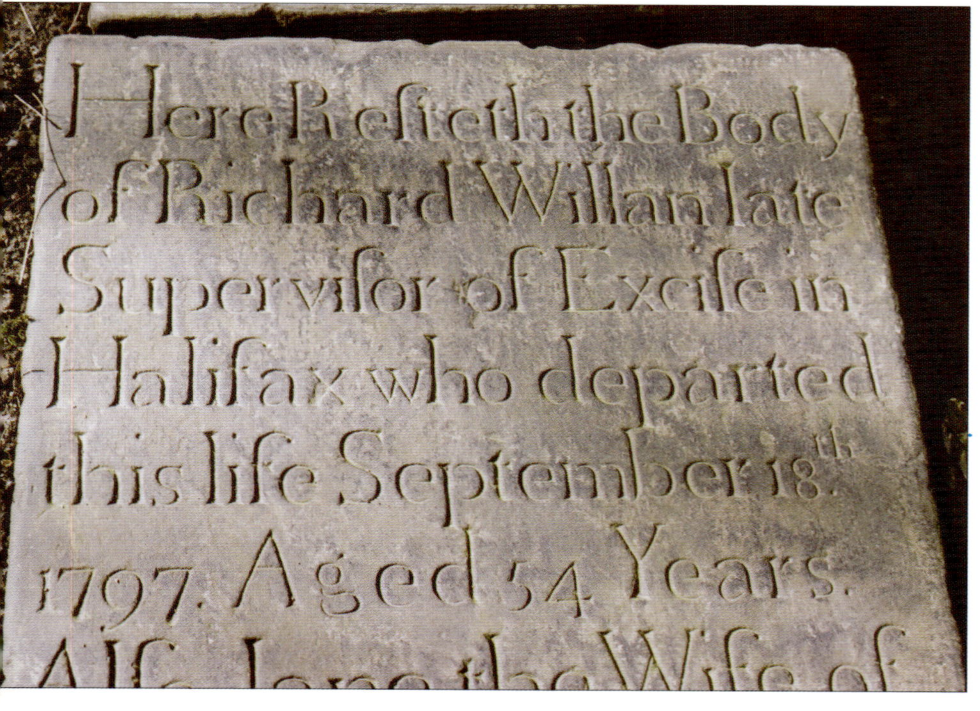

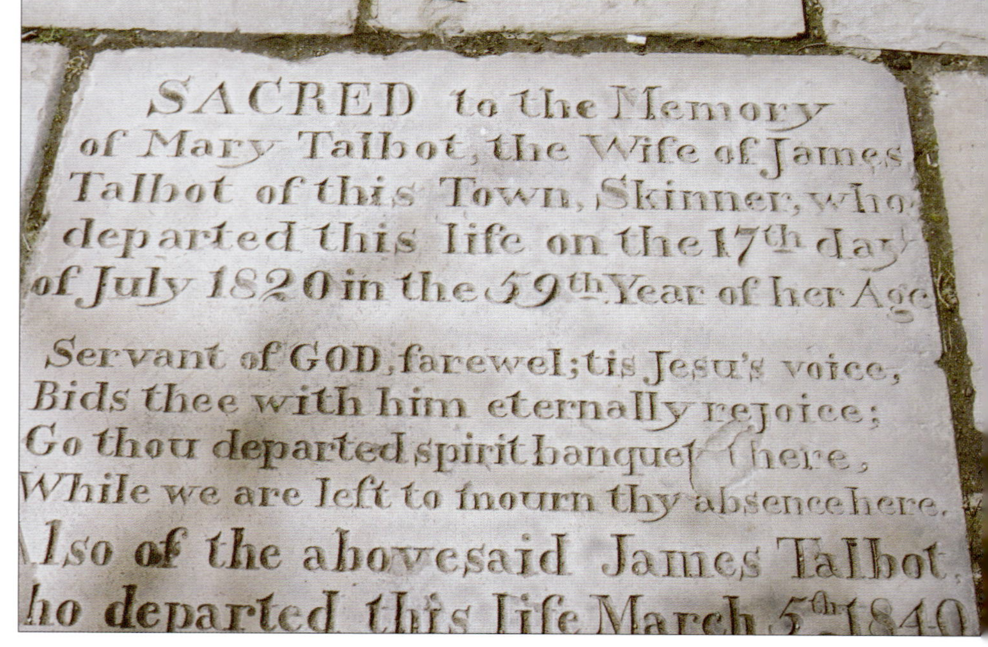

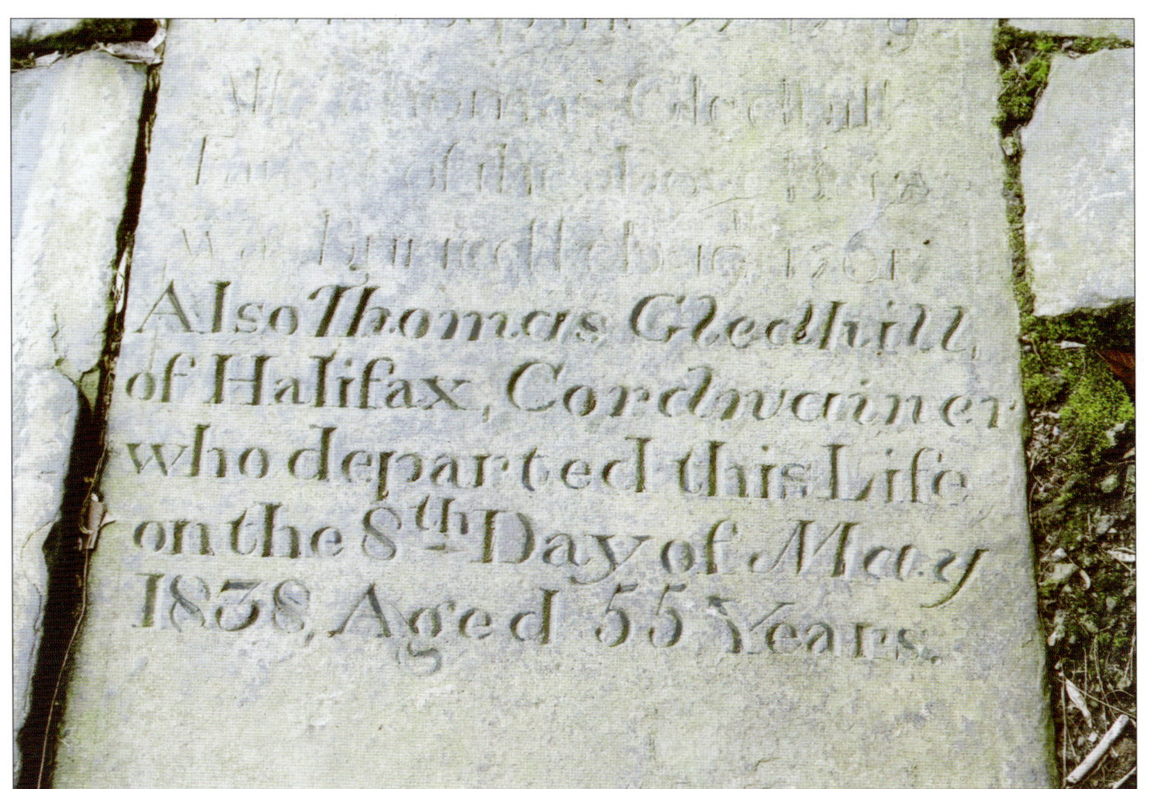

TOP LEFT:
Also THOMAS GLEDHILL of Halifax
CORDWAINER
who departed this Life on the 8th day of May 1838
Aged 55 Years. HALIFAX MINSTER

LOWER LEFT:
Also WILLIAM CROSLAND
BRUSHMAKER
of this town, who died November 30th 1853,
Aged 74 years
ST JOHN'S CHURCH, UPPER BRIGGATE,
LEEDS

LOWER RIGHT:
SACRED TO THE MEMORY OF
WILLIAM SELLERS
BUTCHER
of Bowling, who departed this life the 1st day of
January 1873
Aged 39 Years.

AGAINST ALL ODDS

TOP: *The fire ravaged remains of the Fowler showman's engine 'Renown' after the disastrous fire at Ian Howard's Alton Engineering premises at Kirk Ireton, Derbyshire in 2003.*

BELOW: *'Renown' fully restored at the 2006 Pickering Traction Engine Rally – a fitting tribute to the skills of the Howard brothers and their families and friends who, against all odds, were determined to bring the engine back to life.*

Throughout the history of mankind fire has made a positive contribution to civilization. Heat under the watchful eye and steady hand of the potter, blacksmith and foundry worker has long been at the heart of our cultural and industrial development.

In 1920, the engineering prowess of John Fowler's Steam Plough Works in Leeds brought fire and metallurgy together to create 'Renown', a 17 ton Special Showman's road locomotive.

'Renown' began its working life in the hands of John Murphy of County Durham. Along with its sister engine 'Repulse', 'Renown' hauled Murphy's Scenic Ride to fairground venues throughout the north-east. After passing through several ownerships and phases of neglect and restoration the Howard Brothers became the owners of 'Renown' in 1979. They continued to restore and exhibit this road-going giant of the steam age.

Eighty three years after fire contributed to the creative process of this magnificent machine, it returned to 'Renown' with a more malicious intent. On the 22nd of September 2003 Ian and Gary Howard and their families had to endure a truly awful spectacle as fire attempted to destroy years of restoration work.

The fire which began in a barn at Ian Howard's Alton Engineering premises at Kirk Ireton, Derbyshire, looked like the end not only for 'Renown', but a Burrell traction engine, two transporters, and a section of a fairground galloper ride.

To watch something being destroyed in a fraction of the time it took to create must have been truly distressing. But what followed has rightly become a legend in the annals of rebuilding and restoration. There and then, the Howards and a group of dedicated friends, decided that this would not be the end of 'Renown', and nothing less than complete re-restoration would do – a task that was achieved in an incredible 16 months.

The inspiring story behind 'Renown' is a testament to those, who with unswerving enthusiasm and dedication, choose to give their time through preservation and restoration to secure the legacy of centuries of creativity and skill left to us by our forebears.